WITHER THE FRANC ZONE IN AFRICA?

WITHER THE FRANC ZONE IN AFRICA?

Edited by

Demba Moussa Dembele & Carlos Cardoso

Daraja Press

Published by Daraja Press

For Africaine de Recherche et de Cooperation pour l'Appui au Developpement Endogene (ARCADE) & Council for the Development of Social Science Research in Africa (CODESRIA)

ISBN-13: 978-1508883272
ISBN-10: 1508883270

Project Manager: Firoze Manji
Copy Editor: Andrea Meeson
Design and layout: Tidiane Oumar BA - SOGO BA

CONTENTS

Acronyms & Abbreviations vii

Preface xi

Introduction xiii

Section 1: Conference proceedings 1

Section 2: Papers 39

The CFA franc – A vector of monetary Nazism 40
Nicolas Agbohou

The CFA Franc at the Crossroads: Reforming or Dismantling? 61
Sanou Mbaye

The Franc Zone: An Instrument for Development
or tool of domination? 71
Demba Moussa Dembele

Monetary Integration in West Africa: The Way to the ECOWAS
Single Currency 86
Mohamed Ben Omar Ndiaye

First Steps To Creating The Nilo Currency for Africa 113
Yash Tandon

Comment on Yash Tandon's presentation 131
Lansana Keita

ACRONYMS & ABBREVIATIONS

ACB: AFRICAN CENTRAL BANK

AfDB: AFRICAN DEVELOPMENT BANK

AIB: AFRICAN INVESTMENT BANK

ALBA: BOLIVARIAN ALTERNATIVE FOR THE AMERICAS

AMF: AFRICAN MONETARY FUND

ANMS: AFRICAN NETWORK FOR MONETARY SOVEREIGNTY

ARCADE: AFRICAINE DE RECHERCHE ET DE COOPERATION POUR
            L'APPUI AU DEVELOPPEMENT ENDOGENE

AU: AFRICAN UNION

AUC: AFRICAN UNION COMMISSION

BCEAO: BANQUE CENTRALE DES ETATS DE L'AFRIQUE DE
            L'OUEST (CENTRAL BANK OF WEST AFRICAN STATES)

BEAC: BANQUE DES ETATS DE L'AFRIQUE CENTRALE (BANK
            OF CENTRAL AFRICA STATES)

BLI: BETTER LIFE INDEX

BOAD: BANQUE OUEST AFRICAINE DE DEVELOPPEMENT
            (WEST AFRICAN DEVELOPMENT BANK)

BRICS: BRAZIL, RUSSIA, INDIA, CHINA & SOUTH AFRICA

CACSUP: COMITE AFRICAIN DE COMPLEMENTARITE SCOLAIRE
            ET UNIVERSITAIRE DE PROMOTION

CELAC: COMMUNITY OF LATIN AMERICAN AND
            CARIBBEAN STATES

CEMAC:	COMMUNAUTE ECONOMIQUE ET MONETAIRE DE L'AFRIQUE CENTRALE (ECONOMIC AND MONETARY COMMUNITY OF CENTRAL AFRICA)
CFA:	COOPERATION FINANCIERE AFRICAINE (AFRICAN FINANCIAL COOPERATION)
CODESRIA:	COUNCIL FOR THE DEVELOPMENT OF SOCIAL SCIENCE RESEARCH IN AFRICA
ECA:	ECONOMIC COMMISSION FOR AFRICA
ECB:	EUROPEAN CENTRAL BANK
ECOWAS:	ECONOMIC COMMUNITY OF WEST AFRICAN STATES
EMCP:	ECOWAS MONETARY COOPERATION PROGRAM
EPA:	ECONOMIC PARTNERSHIP AGREEMENT
EU:	EUROPEAN UNION
FASEG:	FACULTY OF ECONOMICS AND MANAGEMENT
FORAM:	FORUM FOR ANOTHER MALI
GDP:	GROSS DOMESTIC PRODUCT
G77:	GROUP OF 77 (OVER 100 COUNTRIES OF THE SOUTH)
HDI:	HUMAN DEVELOPMENT INDEX
HIPC:	HEAVILY INDEBTED POOR COUNTRY
IDEP:	AFRICAN INSTITUTE FOR ECONOMIC DEVELOPMENT AND PLANNING
IMF:	INTERNATIONAL MONETARY FUND
LDCs:	LEAST DEVELOPED COUNTRIES
NATO:	THE NORTH ATLANTIC TREATY ORGANIZATION
OECD:	ORGANIZATION FOR ECONOMIC COOPERATION AND DEVELOPMENT
SAC:	SINGLE AFRICAN CURRENCY

UCAD:	CHEIKH ANTA DIOP UNIVERSITY OF DAKAR
UEMOA:	WEST AFRICAN ECONOMIC AND MONETARY UNION
UGB:	GASTON BERGER UNIVERSITY
UNDP:	UNITED NATIONS DEVELOPMENT PROGRAM
WACH:	WEST AFRICAN CLEARING HOUSE
WAEMU:	WEST AFRICAN ECONOMIC AND MONETARY UNION
WAMA:	WEST AFRICAN MONETARY AGENCY
WAMZ:	WEST AFRICAN MONETARY ZONE
WTO:	WORLD TRADE ORGANIZATION

PREFACE

From 11 to 13 October 2012, at Al Afifa Hotel and at the Cheikh Anta Diop University in Dakar, Senegal, an international conference was held on the future of the CFA franc zone, African countries and the franc zone: Remaining in the trap or opting for monetary independence, under the initiative of the Africaine de Recherche et de Coopération pour l'Appui au Développement Endogène (ARCADE) and the Council for the Development of Social Science Research in Africa (CODESRIA), with the support of the Karibu Foundation (Norway), which provided a grant to that effect.

During the first two days (11 and 12 October) presentations and discussions took place at the Al Afifa Hotel, while the third day (13 October) was dedicated to a meeting of participants with students at the Cheikh Anta Diop University (UCAD) to debate the issue of monetary sovereignty.

Representatives from the African Development Bank (AfDB) and the African Institute for Economic Development and Planning (IDEP) took part in the conference. The government and the National Assembly of Senegal were also represented, as well as the Cheikh Anta Diop University of Dakar (UCAD) and the Gaston Berger University (UGB) of St. Louis.

The conference brought together experts and high-level participants from Africa, Latin America and Europe. Its main objectives were:

  ◆ To demonstrate that the CFA franc is an obstacle to the development of African countries. The operating mechanisms of the franc zone and the monetary policies imposed on those countries are largely responsible for the failure of the CFA franc to be an instrument for development. An illustration of this failure is reflected in the economic and social realities of those countries, almost all of which are ranked either as least developed countries (LDCs) or as heavily indebted poor countries (HIPCs).

♦ To explore alternatives to the current system, either through bold reforms or by abolishing the CFA franc. This alternative is consistent with the view that exiting the trap of the franc zone and creating a sovereign currency are among the indispensable conditions to promote the autonomous development of African countries.

♦ The specific objectives of the conference included, among others:

♦ A review of the global context, characterised by the systemic crisis of capitalism and the questioning of its legitimacy in several regions of the world, particularly in the Global South;

♦ An overview of several attempts at economic and monetary emancipation; going on in other parts of the South, especially in Latin America, and the lessons that African countries can learn from them;

♦ The consequences of the franc zone and its implications for the development of African countries, including the analysis of the latter's economic and social record;

♦ A review of the experiences of countries that gained their monetary sovereignty and the lessons for the creation of a West African currency.

This report summarises the presentations and debates that took place during the conference and highlights its main recommendations.

Demba Moussa Dembele

INTRODUCTION

DEMBA MOUSSA DEMBELE AND CARLOS CARDOSO

This book contains the proceedings of an international conference on the future of the franc zone, which took place in October 2012 in Dakar, Senegal. It was organised by African Research and Cooperation for Supporting Endogenous Development (ARCADE) and the Council for the Development of Social Science Research in Africa (CODESRIA). The meeting was attended by more than 50 participants, including economists and researchers in other disciplines of social sciences, members of social movements, representatives from African institutions, as well as members of the Senegalese National Assembly and government.

The conference took place in two stages. During the first two days, participants heard presentations on the international economic and financial crisis and the situation in the franc zone and African member countries. Rich and sometimes contradictory debates and important recommendations followed these presentations. Thereafter, ARCADE and CODESRIA, in collaboration with Centre Africain du Complimentarite Scolaire, Universitaire et de Promotion (CACSUP), organised a meeting at the Cheikh Anta Diop University (UCAD).

The conference was held in the global context of the systemic crisis of capitalism and the collapse of market fundamentalism. This crisis, likened by some to a 'crisis of civilisation', led to the questioning of neoclassical thought and a growing distrust of its analysis of the problems of the South. Samir Amin (2010) tells us that 'to understand the nature of this crisis, the challenges, and from there imagine the possible contours of the various alternative systems that gradually will emerge from the answers that the dominant forces in place, states and ruling classes, as well as workers and oppressed people, will give them, it is necessary to go beyond the analysis of the unfolding of the financial crisis per se.'[1]

It is in this perspective that numerous calls were made urging countries from the South to rethink their development by exploring other paradigms. In this context, it is sufficient to recall, for example, alternative theories in which the United Nations Economic Commission for Latin America (CEPAL) and the Economic Commission for Africa (ECA) played an important role, demonstrating great independence of thought and action. Given that development is a rather broad topic, in recent decades, new dimensions that were absent in previous discussions have been added to the debates. The latest Latin American proposals related to the concepts of buen vivir (good life) or vivir buen (living well) are certainly among them.[2]

The exploration of new paradigms also referred to the need to question the economic instruments available to African countries to build strong economies and to be able to meet the social needs of their population, of which the currency is one the most important. Created on 26 December 1945, the CFA franc was from the very beginning, directly tied to France's colonial policy in Africa, hence its original name, 'Franc of French African Colonies'. Rethinking development in member countries of the franc zone requires questioning dependency relationships vis-à-vis France, of which monetary agreements are one of the pillars. And that means the end of the franc zone and the replacement of the CFA franc by a sovereign currency, conceived as an instrument of economic and social development for member countries.

The conference contributed important debates on the recurring question of the CFA franc. But beyond the future of the currency, it is the set of relations between France and African countries that needs to be questioned and challenged thoroughly. At stake is the independence and sovereignty of the latter. This was stressed by

---

1. Amin, S. (2010) 'Financial crisis? Systemic crisis ?', CODESRIA, Série de conférences publiques, No. 10.
2 . On the discussions on new development dimensions, see, for instance, Domingues, J.M. (2012), Desarrollo, Periferia y Semiperiferia en la Tercera Fase de la Modernidad Global, CLACSO, Coleccion Sur Sur.

Nicolas Agbohou during the presentation titled 'The CFA franc against Africa' Agbohou reminded us that money is an essential tool for the development of any country and control of it is a fundamental aspect of sovereignty. He described the monetary relations between African countries and France as monetary Nazism, with reference to monetary relations imposed by Nazi Germany in occupied countries during the Second World War. Such a system was characterised by:

♦ The presence of Nazi officers in the heart of the monetary and financial system of the vanquished states and occupied by the Germans
♦ The forced devaluation of the currency of the country conquered by the Germans
♦ The replacement of the local currency by a colonial currency invented by Germany
♦ Free shipping of wealth to Germany from occupied countries through the clearing and trading accounts opened in Berlin.

Being Nazi-inspired, the franc zone violates the sovereignty of African countries, as illustrated by the 1994 devaluation. Indeed, money is one of the most important attributes of a country's sovereignty. Agbohou quoted Edouard Balladur, the former French prime minister, who said: 'Money is not a technical issue but a political one, which affects the sovereignty and independence of nations.'

If, in their respective constitutions, the fifteen African members of the franc zone assert that only the law enacted by parliament 'determines the currency issuance regime', in reality the monetary agreements with France contradict that. In addition to the violation of the sovereignty of African countries, the working mechanisms of the franc zone primarily serve the interests of France

Agbohou concluded that for African member countries to create conditions for development, the only solution is to get out of the franc zone. This, he said, requires:

♦ Issuing a local currency in order to control all its financial circuits and put to work the African labour force

♦ Industrialisation through local processing into finished products for most of its raw materials

♦ Prioritising intra-African trade, to benefit the more than 1 billion citizens on the continent

♦ Promoting strong management of private enterprises, mixed or semi-private and state-owned companies or public companies

♦ Financing by its own means the effective building of its economic, political and military unity.

The presentation by Demba Moussa Dembele, titled 'Franc Zone: instrument of development or tool of domination?' was in the same vein as that of Agbohou. He began by explaining the nature of money beyond its utilitarian functions that one learns in economics textbooks, as a unit of account, medium of exchange and store of value. Dembele claims that money is more than that: it is a social link and the expression of social relations, because it is 'general equivalent' of all goods. Like Agbohou, Dembele said that money is an attribute of a country's sovereignty, like the flag and the national anthem. It is for these reasons that he concluded that the CFA franc is a denial of the sovereignty of African countries. It is an instrument of domination, and as such, it cannot contribute to development.

To buttress his point, Dembele referred to the subordinate relationships between African and French leaders, the working mechanisms of the franc zone and the monetary policies imposed on African Central Banks. Indeed, these monetarist policies prioritise the fight against inflation at the expense of investment and job creation. These are absurd policies, according to Dembele, because they are disconnected from the economic and social realities of the countries on which they are imposed. Based on the above analysis and observations, Dembele showed that the record of the franc zone could only be negative. He noted that 14 of 15 franc zone African member countries are classified as Heavily Indebted Poor Countries (HIPC) by the World Bank and the IMF, and 11 are in the category of the Least Developed Countries (LDCs), according to the United Nations. Not surprisingly, Dembele came to the same conclusion as Agbohou.

Conclusions, however, were not unanimous at the conference. Sanou Mbaye questioned the relevance of calling for the abolition of the CFA franc in his presentation, 'Franc Zone: reform or abolition?' According to Mbaye, it is desirable to maintain the current structure of the franc zone, in case there is a break with the CFA. However, he noted that the issue of the single currency raises complex political, economic and institutional issues. The ongoing crisis in the euro zone is a telling illustration, and Mbaye argued that it would be difficult or impossible to get to the single currency without a federal structure at the political level. Mbaye said that the dismantling of the franc zone could raise enormous difficulties and that African leaders would not support it. He claimed that the call for the break with the franc zone appeared to be primarily driven by African intellectuals in the anti-globalisation movement. Based on these observations, Mbaye made the following proposals:

♦ Set a frank dialogue between those who support maintaining the CFA and the opponents

♦ Review the policy of the Banc Centrale des Etats de l'Afrique de l'Ouest on inflation, which stifles growth

♦ Examine the issue of parity between the CFA franc and the euro.

♦ Review the West African Economic and Monetary Union (UEMOA) convergence criteria that prevents a single currency, due to stringent conditions set for the inflation rate, public debt relative to GDP and the budget deficit

♦ Require an audit of the use of the CFA franc and the franc zone to objectively assess the record.

That said, the debate also focused on the thorny issue of regional integration. A presentation by Mohamed Ben Omar Ndiaye on 'Monetary integration in West Africa: the road to the single currency in ECOWAS' was a case in point. Ndiaye discussed how the ECOWAS space is presented as encompassing two types of currency areas: the CFA zone and the non-CFA zone, composed of several currencies, including the Nigerian naira and the Ghanaian cedi. A merger of the two areas was considered for 2015, but the deadline was pushed to 2020. According to Ndiaye, the economic and monetary integration in Africa must be seen as an imperative for both promoting development and dealing more effectively with external shocks brought about by globalisation. It is in this context that the ECOWAS member countries should agree to work toward the creation of a single currency.

Ndiaye placed the process of monetary integration in the theory of optimum currency areas, developed by Robert Mundell. A currency area has the following characteristics:

- The exchange rate between the currencies that compose it is fixed
- Currencies are convertible to each other
- Foreign exchange reserves are centralised
- There is a common Central Bank and common economic policy bodies.

After exposing further developments of Mundell's theory by authors, such as McKinnon, Peter B. Kennen and others, Ndiaye focused on the costs and benefits of a monetary zone. The costs would include the abandonment of the use of the exchange rate in the event of exogenous shocks, and the loss of autonomy in monetary policy and even fiscal policy. As for benefits, they would include the elimination of speculation on the exchange rate, the costs of managing external reserves and improving the cash value of the currency.

Referring to the experience of the euro zone, Ndiaye noted that studies showed that the UEMOA did not meet the criteria of an optimum currency area. UEMOA was rather based on economic, financial and political criteria. Although UEMOA does not meet the criteria, the adoption of a common currency promotes compliance with certain convergence criteria, such as the inflation rate or budget deficit ceilings.

Analysing the implications of the ECOWAS monetary cooperation programme, Ndiaye noted that harmonisation of monetary, financial and payment policies was seen as a crucial step in the implementation of the ECOWAS Treaty. But the existence of eight different and non-convertible currencies was a major obstacle to achieving this goal. To overcome this obstacle, monetary cooperation was established through the West Africa Clearing House (WACH) and the Multilateral Mechanism for Compensation of ECOWAS. These two mechanisms should help countries use their own currencies in intra-ECOWAS transactions, allowing them to save foreign exchange. They should also help to simplify the settlement of trade transactions through a multilateral netting system.

But delays and procrastination were noted in the implementation of this programme. Therefore, a new approach was adopted in 2008. It offered a choice between three options: 1) the 'big bang', which is an option based on the leaders' political decision; 2) the prior execution of prescribed eligibility criteria; and 3) at least 60 per cent of ECOWAS's GDP must meet the convergence criteria of the first rank. Examination of these three options led the convergence council to ask the ECOWAS commission to conduct a feasibility study to determine the best option to go to the single currency. In this context, a roadmap was adopted from 2010 to 2020, with specific well-defined goals.

In conclusion, Ndiaye noted that progress has been made in many areas but there is still some way to go to reach the single currency. However, he remained convinced that the benefits of the single currency were more significant than the financial costs. The ECOWAS countries would be well advised to adopt a single currency, essential to the pulse of truly dynamic development in region.

Beyond regional integration, some delegates to the conference believed in a single currency for the continent as a whole. Yash Tandon defended this position in his presentation titled, 'Steps to Establishing the African currency: the NILO' (a reference to the Nile, the river that waters Egypt, Ethiopia, Sudan, Uganda and other African countries). Tandon argued that the francophone countries have the CFA in common, but not a common currency, because having one's own currency would imply having control over it. He said that Africa should have currency that is not convertible and with capital controls. He added that money is a weapon of war par excellence, and the CFA is a currency of occupation. The economy created by such occupation involved a politics by other means. In the colonial system, when the coloniser settled, he controlled the commodity and currency. This is how there was export of capital from Africa to develop the West. Africa must now have its own economy in the policy framework, including its own currency, the nilo . The conditions for success of the nilo are, among others:

- Learn from the experience of other countries in South
- Overcome barriers between African countries and move toward a customs union
- Establish a regional monetary agreement with exchange rate regulations, a regional bank funded by Africa.
- Close all the channels through which the savings of African populations are externalised
- Review the cooperation agreements and bilateral treaties that are obstacles to African development
- Put an embargo on Economic Partnership Agreements (EPAs) and negotiate on its own terms
- Link the Bolivarian Alternative of the Americas (ALBA) and Africa
- Speak with one voice in international fora.

In conclusion, political leaders, business decision makers, sub-regional institutions, researchers, social movements and media that can influence the debate on this issue, should be informed of the conclusions and recommendations of the conference.

African Research and Cooperation for Supporting Endogenous Development and CODESRIA thank all participants, especially those who presented papers, the discussants and all commentators. We also extend special thanks to the members of government, honourable members of parliament and representatives of African institutions, who agreed to attend the conference and take part in discussions.

Our sincere thanks to CACSUP and its Director, Ibrahima Sarr Eloi, and to all the students who participated in the meeting held at the Cheikh Anta Diop University. Finally, ARCADE expresses its deepest and most sincere gratitude to the Karibu Foundation, whose financial support made the conference and the publication of its proceedings possible.

WITHER THE FRANC ZONE IN AFRICA?

Section 1

Conference Proceedings

WITHER THE FRANC ZONE IN AFRICA?

CONFERENCE PROCEEDINGS

OPENING SESSION

The opening session of the conference was chaired by the Hon. Haoua Dia Thiam, MP of the National Assembly of Senegal, accompanied by Demba Moussa Dembele, the President of ARCADE, Carlos Cardoso, the Director of the CODESRIA Research Department, and Coumba Ndoffène Diouf, a researcher at CODESRIA.

Dembele welcomed the participants and introduced the conference in the context of challenging the development models imposed by Western countries on developing countries and the failure of the dominant paradigm, as illustrated by the systemic crisis of global capitalism, which is likened to a 'crisis of civilisation'. Dembele argued that developing countries in general, and African countries in particular, need to rethink their development by deconstructing the dominant discourse on development that is based on a supposedly universal Western model. African countries, especially those using the CFA franc, should acknowledge the moves to emancipate the South from the domination and resource plundering of the former colonial powers and their multinational corporate partners. Indeed, these countries should exit the franc zone, which is one of the most enduring symbols of economic domination and disenfranchisement.

Carlos Cardoso exposed the main challenges facing African countries, including chronic unemployment, endemic poverty, food insecurity, poor infrastructure and environmental degradation. These challenges are compounded by poor political leadership, which bears some responsibility for the failure of development policies since independence. He noted that in 1970, Côte d'Ivoire and Morocco had roughly the same level of development. But 40 years later, life expectancy in Côte d'Ivoire has fallen by 38 per cent, while in Morocco it has increased by 20 per cent. Cardoso argued that this difference can be explained by, among other things, the different development pathways followed by the two countries. But the example of Côte d'Ivoire reflects a situation which must be reviewed in-depth. Hence the need for Africa to reinvent its development in order to join the group of prosperous nations.

In her opening remarks, Haoua Dia Thiam said that currency is at the heart of the economic independence of African countries and it is imperative that they come out from under the tutelage of western countries and develop their own models based on endogenous values.

Coumba Ndoffène Diouf reviewed the conference agenda and process in detail. All deliberations would be conducted in plenary sessions. Each session would consist of presenters and discussants. The role of discussants was to make critical comments on the presentations and enrich them. After comments by discussants, the floor would be opened for comment from the floor.

DAY ONE
GLOBAL ECONOMIC CRISIS AND DIAGNOSIS OF THE FRANC ZONE

The first part of the day was dedicated to the analysis of ongoing changes in the global context following the collapse of market fundamentalism and their impact on developing countries. Analysis and perspectives from Latin America and Africa were presented. The second part of the day was reserved for a thorough analysis of the origins and development of the franc zone.

PLENARY SESSION ONE:
TOWARD A NEW INTERNATIONAL MONETARY AND FINANCIAL SYSTEM?

Chair:
Boubacar Barry*, Professor, Cheikh Anta Diop University (UCAD)
Speakers:
Pedro Paez, Ecuador
François Ndgengwe, Cameroon/France
Discussants:
Moubarak Lo, Deputy Director of the President's Cabinet, Senegal,
Felwine Sarr, Dean of the Faculty of Economics, Gaston Berger University,
Saint-Louis, Senegal
sitting in for Mamadou Lamine Loum, the former prime minister of Senegal

PEDRO PAEZ AND FRANCOIS NDENGWE : BUILDING A NEW INTERNATIONAL FINANCIAL SYSTEM

Paez began by analysing the origins of the current global economic and financial crisis. He went on to review its implications for countries of the South before outlining solutions available to these countries, with particular emphasis on efforts underway in Latin America.

The current crisis of capitalism is very different from what the world has experienced in the past. This is why it cannot be explained by the cycle theories, proposed by eminent economists, such as Kondratieff and Leontief, among others. At issue is a 'crisis of civilisation', because it spares no aspect of economic, social and political life, and it deeply challenges conventional analyses of growth and development. Furthermore, it is fundamentally changing the relationship between the South and the North. This 'crisis of civilisation' is partly due to the ferocity and speed of the transformation of the capitalist economy. Already, in 1960, a crisis of overproduction was looming. This was followed by neoliberal globalisation and the financialisation of the economy, the consequences of which were quasi-permanent economic instability, social polarisation, a widening gap between rich and poor countries, and growing inequalities between populations of the North and the South.

The gap between the real economy and the financialised economy is clearly indicated by a global public and private debt estimated at roughly $250 trillion and a global GDP of a mere $63 trillion. Such a gap explains why the same asset is sometimes sold more than ten times. There are various other key factors influencing the gap. These include: financial liberalisation that encourages rampant speculation, which is the root cause of the current global financial crisis; the rapid growth of the South as opposed to low growth and stagnation in developed countries; the unsustainable levels of the debt incurred by banks and households; the gap between the needs of households and disposable income, the former being three times higher than the latter during the past ten years; the progressive decline in the economic hegemony of northern countries; the concentration of economic power, which perpetuates an increasingly arrogant and immoral financial oligarchy; and trade and currency wars in the race for economic hegemony.

To illustrate the enormous concentration of economic and financial power in the hands of a small number of companies and banks, one need only consider that a mere 147 transnational companies control 40 per cent of the global GDP, 50 of which control the equivalent of 110 per cent of the GDP of the United States ($14.7 trillion). Banks are among these companies and they accumulate huge losses, yet these are not reflected in their balance sheets. For instance, GP Morgan bank accumulated $83 billion off-balance sheet losses. In total, the US Government in the period 2007-2009 used nearly $29 trillion, more than double the country's GDP, to bail out banks, with mixed results. Yet, the US Federal Reserve and other central banks in the world have fewer and fewer resources to support their economies. All these factors combine to create a catastrophic situation in terms of confidence.

The issue of insolvency, due to the fall in liquidity, leads to global money wars, which serve to make southern countries prisoners of the dominant system. Solutions proposed in the north to address the international economic and financial crisis are doomed to fail because they are the same solutions that have failed previously, and they do not address the root causes of the problem. For example, despite the massive injection of liquidity by the US Federal Reserve, which alone poured $16 trillion into the US economy – an amount higher than the country's GDP – between 1 December 2007 and July 2010, the economy struggled to recover from the crisis. It continues to provide liquidity to the chagrin of the country's main trading partners.

Countries in the West tend to favour the multiplication of local wars and outbreaks of tension against the South and its allies as way to get out of the crisis. Several examples illustrate this analysis. The first is the ongoing tension in the Middle East, including the war in Syria and threats against Iran, all orchestrated by the US and its allies. Another is the destabilisation of African countries, including western aggression against Libya and the protracted war in the Democratic Republic of Congo. Also, the North Atlantic Treaty Organisation (NATO), headed by the US, is encircling Russia by enlisting in its membership some of that country's most hostile neighbours. The fourth example is the strategy of the US to contain China's rise in Asia/Pacific and elsewhere in the world.

In conclusion, the way out of the crisis for developing countries, including China and Russia, is through south-south solidarity, the building of broad coalitions and resistance to the western strategies described above. The example of Latin America is instructive. Countries in this region have been quite successful in freeing themselves from the trap of foreign domination through political will and determination. It is incumbent on countries of the South to move away from the crisis-stricken capitalist system, of which they have been the main victims for more than five centuries. A new type of development, based on the sovereignty of peoples and nations, is recommended. This would include new monetary and financial systems as tools for wealth creation along with a banking service for autonomous development. Latin American institutions, such as the Bolivarian Development Bank and the Bank of the South, are good examples. They promote:

- ◆ Mechanisms of financing economic and social development at odds with those of the International Monetary Fund (IMF)

- ◆ A new vision of sub-regional integration with South-South transactions that do not use either the dollar or the euro

- ◆ A new system for sovereign loan guarantee and a new clearing system

- ◆ Instruments for local resource mobilisation with a new international reserve currency

- ◆ Tools to promote a shift in the epistemological development framework

- ◆ A financial system founded on macroeconomic frameworks that encourage coherent articulation between various central banks, and better monetary and financial cooperation

- ◆ Instruments to fight more effectively against the global financial oligarchy.

François Ndengwe, Chairman, African Advisory Board, Paris: How Could Africans Become the Richest in the 21st Century?

Ndengwe emphasised the failure of contemporary economics to foresee and solve crises. He illustrated this by discussing the subprime crisis of 2008, which triggered a financial storm and brought the entire world into its vortex. In the US, a country full of prize-winning economists, no one was able to find solutions to this crisis due to the nature of the neoclassical growth model, which does not account for the reality of daily life in any country.

The failure of the neoclassical growth model is illustrated by the current situation faced by the US and European countries, which are mired in deep crisis that is not only economic, but also social and political. For instance, in the US, the huge public and household debt means that companies and banks have mortgaged the country's real economy. It is a country at the helm of the western world that is an advanced state of decline.

This decline is even more pronounced in Europe. Even Germany, the driver of the euro zone, is affected by an aging population and a subsequent drain on its pension system. In other European countries, including France and Britain, the economic crisis continues to wreak havoc, while Greece, Portugal and Spain are in an increasingly untenable situation because of the drastic measures of austerity associated with the repayment of their respective debt.

Another example of the inability of neoclassical economics to account for reality is how it measures the wealth of nations as GDP. The GDP does not provide a full picture of the wealth of a nation, because it does not take into account all opportunities for men and women to develop their full potential. Although the Human Development Index (HDI) proposed by the UNDP is a better indicator, it is still limited. There is also the Better Life Index (BLI), proposed by the Organisation for Economic Cooperation and Development (OECD), which counters both the GDP and the HDI. Despite these alternative instruments, the GDP remains the benchmark for measuring national wealth.

By adopting other than the GDP measure of development and wealth, Africa could experience rapid development and become a world economic power during this century. To be avoided are the illusions that go along with the high growth rates of African countries celebrated by international development agencies and western neoliberal media. Indeed, such growth rates do not create jobs, nor do they contribute to improving the living conditions of the overwhelming majority of the population, as shown in the ranking of African countries at the bottom of the UNDP human development index.

Africans, therefore, must reclaim their development policies and give new meaning to the concepts of development and national wealth. It is only under these conditions that they can radically transform the current situation on the continent. One of the instruments that could help Africa achieve this goal is a sovereign currency to replace the multiple currencies, such as the CFA franc. These currencies are the remnants of colonialism and therefore obstacles to economic and social progress. An epistemological shift to adopt a definition of economic development that is more appropriate for Africa and its people is recommended. This would entail:

- Rethinking economic development from the bottom-up
- Prioritising the values that will ensure social stability by giving culture its rightful position and setting new conditions of existence
- Developing a new social contract, inverting the problem and defining what kind of society we want
- Taking stock of 50 years of the franc zone, which would allow African countries to reach a well-grounded conclusion whether to leave or stay in this monetary arrangement.

COMMENTS BY DISCUSSANTS

Mubarak Lô

The world is facing massive systemic risks illustrated by the huge gap between the global GDP ($63 trillion) and the value of derivatives ($1,500 trillion), and the amount of worldwide debt ($200 trillion). This explains, among other things, why all the bailouts in western countries have failed, and only reinforces pessimism about the possibility of resolving the global financial and economic crisis through conventional means.

While northern countries are entangled in increasingly intractable problems, we are witnessing the emergence of economies of larger countries in the South, which tends to offset the series of recessions in industrialised countries. This emergence signals the beginning of a more diversified and multipolar world economy.

In this global context of political and economic change, Africa is trying to find a way of its own. This is illustrated by the decision to establish an African Central Bank (ACB), an African Monetary Fund (AMF), and an African Investment Bank (AIB) – decisions that reflect an awareness by African leaders of the need to speed up sub-regional and continental economic integration. Monetary policies, must be backed by a certain discipline, with moderate inflation rates that do not stifle economic growth and job creation.

Felwine Sarr

The challenge for African and other developing countries is how to adopt autonomous macroeconomic policies and find local sources of financing. To achieve this goal those countries and their leaders need to think by themselves, which means adopting fundamental epistemological shifts. Such shifts involve promoting and protecting endogenous mechanisms of knowledge production. There is a need to challenge the concept of development as promoted by the dominant paradigm.

Regarding the franc zone, asymmetric shocks between member countries tend to make monetary policy, as advocated by the rules of the franc zone, less effective. As for the future of the CFA, there is a need for a comprehensive and in-depth analysis of not only the economic and financial implications, but also the geopolitical implications of an exit from that zone by African countries.

Conclusion

Following the comments by the two discussants, other participants revisited some important aspects of the presentations. The following key points were noted:

♦ The world is undergoing fundamental changes that require a rethinking of the concept of development in the South.

♦ The current crisis of capitalism is so pervasive that many consider it to be a 'crisis of civilisation'. This entails profound global economic, social and political transformation.

♦ The crisis in the north is likely to worsen and have far-reaching consequences because the interests of the financial markets have taken precedence over those of the real economy.

♦ Many developing countries, particularly in Latin America, have taken new paths that enabled them to recover sovereignty over their resources, and economic and social policies. Africa must learn from the example of Latin America and the two continents must join forces and support one another to overcome foreign domination and find original ways of developing their full potential to become world economic powers.

♦ The fate of the African continent has been decided for more than five centuries by the outside world, most recently by the World Bank, IMF and WTO. This must come to an end and Africa must regain control over its destiny. The African Union is proposing to build new African economic and financial institutions that would help the continent recover its sovereignty over its development process.

♦ Rethinking the concept of development includes challenging the concept of measurement of GDP as a way of calculating the wealth of a nation.

♦ The concept of 'impoverishing growth' has been given as an illustration of the disconnect between growth and development, since there can be growth without significant job creation, thus without a real impact on people's lives

♦ The franc zone was and remains an instrument of domination. It violates the economic sovereignty of African countries. Worse still, it violates their constitutions. Currency is a political issue because it is an attribute of a country's sovereignty. It is a symbol of power. It is a social link and permeates all activities in a society. This conviction is one of the driving forces behind the campaign for the abolition of the franc zone.

♦ A compelling reason for the abolition of the franc zone is the monetary policies associated with CFA countries. These are choking public investments and job creation as a result of a monetarist credo imposed by the European Central Bank.

♦ In the Economic Community of the West African States (ECOWAS), the asymmetric adjustments between anglophone countries with flexible exchange rates and francophone countries with a fixed exchange rate could be another obstacle to achieving the objective of a single currency.

PLENARY SESSION TWO

THE FRANC ZONE, 50 YEARS AFTER: WHAT RESULTS?

Chair:
Aminata Diaw, CODESRIA
Presenters:
Nicolas Agbohou, Professor,
Demba Moussa Dembele, President, ARCADE
Discussants:
Marème Ndoye, Professor, Department of Economics, UCAD
Samba Ka, Consultant

THE CFA AGAINST AFRICA
Nicolas Agbohou

Professor Agbohou asserted that money is an essential tool for the development of any country and also for its control. Those who control the currency are more powerful than the lawmakers and other politicians. In this regard, he quoted Nathan Rothschild: 'Give me control of a nation's money supply and I don't care about who makes its laws.'

A parallel can be drawn between the franc zone and the monetary Nazism that was applied in occupied France during the Second World War. The latter system was characterised by:

♦ The presence of Nazi officers at the heart of the financial and monetary system of states occupied by the Germans

♦ The forced devaluation of the currency of states under occupation

♦ The replacement of the local currency with a colonial German currency

♦ Free supply of Germany with the wealth from occupied countries through the clearing and transactions accounts opened in Berlin.

Thus, after the contribution of Africans to the liberation of France, as a 'reward', General de Gaulle applied the Nazi monetary system to African colonies by creating the franc zone and the CFA franc (CFA originally meaning "colonies françaises d'Afrique" or French colonies in Africa). In fact, one finds the same type of relationships that Nazi Germany applied to France in the relations of the latter with African countries. This is illustrated by the four pillars that govern the franc zone: 1) the transactions accounts; 2) the fixed exchange rate between the CFA franc and the French franc and now the Euro; 3) the free flow of capital between France and African countries; and 4) the centralisation of African foreign exchange reserves, half of which are deposited in France. All these mechanisms are tools in the hands of France, which enable it to control the economies of African countries and plunder their resources.

The CFA franc was created on December 25, 1945 pursuant to Article 3 of Decree No. 45-0136 and published on 26 December 1945 in the French official gazette. General de Gaulle was its founding father. The CFA franc is printed in Chamalières, near Clermont-Ferrand (Auvergne). The creation of the CFA was a clear and deliberate violation of the constitutions and sovereignty of African states, because money is a symbol of sovereignty. This is starkly confirmed in the words of Edouard Balladur, a former prime minister of France: 'currency is not a technical issue, but a political one, which affects the sovereignty and independence of Nations.'

Indeed, constitutionally, to issue money is a sovereign right that falls within the exclusive jurisdiction of the people through their institutions. And in their respective constitutions, the 15 African member countries of the franc zone state that only the act passed by Parliament 'shall determine the regime of issuing currency'. However, this assertion is contradicted by the monetary agreements signed with France. Indeed, the violation of the sovereignty of African states is notable in the functioning of all institutions of the franc zone, including the summit of heads of state and the council of ministers.

Since the creation of the Franc Zone in 1945, France has used part of the foreign currencies earned by African countries for itself. In addition, it continues to deny African countries the power to issue their own currency. Furthermore, France uses the export earnings of African countries to cover part of its budget deficits and repay a portion of its external debt. African countries also help to pay for the deficit of the French balance of payment

In conclusion African countries that are members of the franc zone and are committed to development have no choice but to abandon the CFA. The creation of a single currency and domestic processing of raw materials is integral to generate wealth and create jobs, especially for the youth. To achieve this, African countries must create the African Single Currency in accordance with the following internal rules of conduct:

- High degree of local processing of raw materials
- African exports dominated by finished products processed on African soil
- Securing the African single currency with the value of African raw materials

- A moderate rate of inflation in line with development priorities

- A sustainable outstanding external debt compatible with the needs of the economy

- A tax ratio compatible with economic and social priorities.

Furthermore, in order to develop autonomously, Africa must:
- Issue a currency of its own to control all financial circuits and finance projects aimed at creating jobs

- Industrialise through local processing of most raw materials into finished products

- Give priority to intra-African trade to support a burgeoning continental population, which is expected to number two billion by 2050

- Finance through its own means the effective realisation of a unified region at economic, political and military levels.

FRANC ZONE: INSTRUMENT OF DEVELOPMENT OR TOOL OF DOMINATION?
Demba Moussa Dembele,

Dembele argued that the nature of a currency goes beyond the utilitarian functions that one learns about in economics textbooks. Money is a social link and the expression of social relations as a general equivalent. It is an attribute of sovereignty of a country just like the flag and national anthem. That is why one of the first acts of a country that gains its freedom and independence is to create its own currency. Thus, the CFA franc is a denial of African countries' sovereignty. It is an instrument of their domination and as such, it cannot contribute to development.

African leaders who left or attempted to leave the franc zone in the early 1960s or later were either subjected to merciless economic and financial wars (Sekou Toure in Guinea), or murdered (Sylvanus Olympio of Togo), or victims of coups (Modibo Keita in Mali). Thus, the franc zone is a symbol of permanent humiliation for the leaders of countries that remain in this monetary zone, as further evidenced by the 1994 devaluation of the CFA franc (by 50 per cent), another act imposed on African leaders against their will.

Apart from the subordinate relationships between African and French leaders, the monetary policies imposed on African Central Banks are a mortgage on African countries' development. Indeed, the monetarist-inspired policies rather prioritise the fight against inflation at the expense of investment and job creation. Such a policy is all the more absurd because the sources of inflation in African countries have nothing to do with excess money supply. In addition to imported inflation, they are related to the structure of African economies, such as the low level of supply relative to demand, particularly in food products. Moreover, the obsession with inflation of the central banks of the franc zone member countries is not justified by the development needs of those countries. Consider a study by the African Development Bank (AfDB) that shows that even double-digit inflation may be a source of growth without jeopardising the macroeconomic equilibrium. This study reviews several examples in Africa and in other countries.

The record of the franc zone is very negative for African countries. Apart from the low inflation rate, as a result of monetarist policies, all the other so-called benefits of the franc zone have not been proven. The existence of a common currency doesn't promote the integration of member countries whose trade is less than 15 per cent of their total trade within West African Economic and Monetary Union (WAEMU) and less than 10 per cent within the Economic and Monetary Union of Central Africa (CEMAC). The growth rates in these countries are no better than those of other

African countries with their own currencies, most of which are able to attract more foreign investment, despite high levels of inflation. Furthermore, the free transfer of capital between France and African countries opens the door to capital flight and deprives the latter of their savings and valuable foreign currencies gained by the toil of their farmers and other workers. Despite its excess cash flow, the private banking system in African countries does not contribute to the financing of the economy. As a result of the above policies, 14 of the 15 African member countries of the franc zone are ranked among the HIPCs by the World Bank and the IMF, and 11 of those are in the category of (LDCs), according to the United Nations Development Program UNDP.

In light of this dismal picture and in order to embark on the path to autonomous development, there is the need to break with the system of the franc zone and create a sovereign currency. The fight to exit the franc zone is part of a broader process aimed at rethinking development in Africa in light of the collapse of the founding myths of capitalism, and the failure of more than 50 years of neo-colonial policies.

COMMENTS BY DISCUSSANTS

Marème Ndoye

It is true that the record and impact of the CFA franc have been negative, but it has at least one positive aspect, in the sense that it brought together 15 African countries. This is why I have trouble with the title of this conference, which implies that the franc zone is a trap. I believe there are groups, such as traders and expatriates who have interests in maintaining the CFA franc. We must take into account this reality in the debate on the future of the franc zone.

Money is a complex phenomenon. So, ending the CFA franc will require not only political courage from leaders, but also, and above all, a good development strategy with a sovereign currency as an instrument. Monetary independence should be based on a strategic plan, which should consider the following:

♦ The national, sub-regional and international economic context

♦ The policy of macroeconomic and financial stability

♦ The involvement of all economic and social actors in decision-making

♦ The relationship between money, growth, inflation, employment and balance of payments

♦ The importance of cultural factors, such as people's attitude toward development

♦ Establishing priorities leading to an optimal choice in the allocation of resources.

Samba Ka

In my opinion, there is a problem of approach – Agbohou developed a clinical approach, while Dembele developed a massive approach. But both lead to the same conclusion, which is a radical solution, namely the rejection of the CFA franc and the creation of a sovereign currency. I agree with such a solution, and that the CFA franc, which was imposed by the colonial order, remains a symbol of the balkanisation of Africa. But I am disappointed that there is not an expert who supports the CFA franc participating in this debate.

We seem to be wedded to the CFA system, probably because we have known nothing else since independence. Furthermore, a special interest group has developed around the CFA franc, especially local interests with the trading bourgeoisie and the Europeanised petty bourgeoisie. These groups benefit from the franc zone.

For example, in 1990 there was a large outflow of currencies operated by the bureaucratic bourgeoisie to France. I think that many executives at the BCEAO do not have the required training, and especially the awareness needed to understand the challenges of maintaining the CFA franc.

I agree that if one analyses the monetary arrangement of the franc zone, it does not reflect the fundamentals of African economies. Transactions accounts, where part of African foreign exchange reserves are deposited, tend to deprive African countries of precious resources. We must break with the colonial logic that is suicidal for our people and end the CFA franc. However, to get there, we must further examine the subject with in-depth studies to better understand the implications and the best approach.

Conclusion

After the presentations and comments by discussants, the following conclusions were drawn:

- The idea of rejecting the franc zone and the CFA franc is not new. It is a struggle that began in the early years of independence and remains an obstacle to development in African member countries. After more than 50 years and the dismal record of the franc zone, this imperative is even more compelling.

- It is necessary to envisage all possible scenarios once out of the franc zone: economic interests, class analysis, relations with the rest of the world, etc.

- It is time to deny outside forces the right to decide for Africans on such a strategic issue as the currency. It is a matter of political and economic sovereignty

- The struggle must not be confined to intellectual and political circles only. It must be owned by the people and social movements.

DAY TWO
EXPLORING ALTERNATIVES

Whereas, the first day was focused on the diagnosis of the franc zone, the second day was dedicated to exploring alternatives for African member countries. Thus, one of the two sessions discussed the advantages and disadvantages of leaving the franc zone, and the other session outlined the conditions required for the creation of a sovereign currency in West Africa, and at continental level.

PLENARY SESSION ONE
TOWARD MONETARY INDEPENDENCE?

Chair:
Dr Cherif Salif Sy
Presenter:
M. Sanou Mbaye, economist and essayist, former senior economist at the African Development Bank (AfDB
Discussants:
Boubacar Barry (UCAD)
Maurice Fahe (Côte d'Ivoire).

Cherif Sy opened this plenary session with an overview of the first day of presentations and discussion. He noted that the second day would be dedicated to exploring strategies and policies that can help African countries recover their monetary sovereignty and achieve autonomy in their development policies.

THE FRANC ZONE: REFORM OR ABOLITION?
Sanou Mbaye

Mbaye argued that in the event of a break with the franc zone it would be desirable to maintain the current structure of African monetary cooperation. But the issue of a single currency raises political, economic and institutional complexities. The ongoing crisis in the eurozone is one telling illustration. Without a federal structure in place it will be difficult, if not impossible to achieve a single currency.

The idea of abandoning the franc zone seems to be mainly promoted by African intellectuals in the alter globalist movement. In reality an exit from this monetary system could create enormous challenges, and it is questionable whether African leaders would be in favour. We also need further dialogue proponents and opponents of the CFA franc. The following should also be addressed:

♦ There is a need to review the allocation of foreign exchange reserves between France and African countries in order to increase the benefits to member countries.

♦ Review the policy of the BCEAO on inflation, which stifles growth. Question the fixed parity between the CFA franc and the euro. The strong euro may be acceptable for member countries that mutually exchange up to 80 per cent of total trade, but not for African countries whose mutual trade is between 10 and 15 per cent.

♦ Review the convergence criteria of WAEMU, which prevent having a single currency, because of the stringent conditions attached to the inflation rate, public debt relative to GDP and the budget deficit

♦ Request an audit of the use of the CFA franc to assess more objectively its record and draw well-founded conclusions as to whether to abolish it or not.

COMMENTS BY DISCUSSANTS

Maurice Fahe

I support the idea of dismantling the franc zone, because it has proven completely negative for African countries. But, I agree that the process is complex and we should approach it with caution and deeper reflection. The audit proposed by Mbaye could be a useful tool to make a decision based on real facts and a solid analysis. Furthermore, our debate should move from theory to practice by examining the real implications of dismantling the franc zone for African member economies and the impact it would have on the day to day lives of the majority of people in those countries.

Debate on this very important and sensitive issue should not remain within intellectual and political circles. It should be owned by social movements and the people. Conversation between intellectuals and social movements is essential for a breakthrough on this issue.

Boubacar Barry

The issue of monetary sovereignty should be considered in the context of regional integration, as the notion of nation-state is against federalism, which is a system highly valued by the proponents of Pan-Africanism. It is necessary to revisit the issue of large blocs not only with regard to the monetary issue, but also for the reconstruction of solidarity among African countries. However on the issue of monetary sovereignty, among others, it is necessary to pay attention to evidence and reality.

Money is not an end in itself, but a means to put to work the forces of a nation and create wealth within it. That is why it is essential to put an end to monetary colonisation and get together to create a sovereign currency at regional and continental levels.

Beyond solidarity among African countries, it is desirable to strengthen solidarity between countries in the South. The establishment of a Bank of the South, would provide financing for developing countries and put an end to the intervention of the Bretton Woods institutions in Africa and elsewhere.

Conclusions

After the presentation and comments, a general debate took place and led to the following conclusions:

♦ The continuing use of the CFA franc is partly due to the fact that most leaders of member countries think they derive their legitimacy not from their own people, but also from abroad, especially from former colonial powers and other western countries.

♦ The longevity of the CFA franc is also due to the fact that the mentality of the majority of Africans, including some intellectuals and leaders, is yet to be decolonised. Decolonising the minds of African citizens is an urgent task which calls for the structural reform of curricula in schools and universities.

♦ It is necessary to cut the umbilical cord of domination with the West and dismantle a currency inherited from colonisation such as the CFA franc. The dismantling of the franc zone is the only option, and Africans must agree to make the necessary sacrifices to free themselves. There is no other solution, lest they accept perpetual domination.

♦ The proposal for accounting and financial, economic and legal auditing of the franc zone can help to substantiate this requirement.

♦ Money is part of a country's defence and security, which are two powerful symbols of national sovereignty. African countries should strive to consolidate their independence and recover their sovereignty. In this respect, they should no longer accept budget support of the European Union.

PLENARY SESSION TWO
TOWARD AN AFRICAN CURRENCY

Chair:

Carlos Cardoso, CODESRIA

Presenters:

Mohamed Ben Omar Ndiaye, Director General of the West African Monetary Agency (WAMA)

Yash Tandon, former executive director of the South Centre, Geneva

Discussants:

Lansana Keita, Professor, University of Ibadan, Nigeria

Nicolas Agbohou, Professor,

MONETARY INTEGRATION IN WEST AFRICA: PROGRESS TOWARD THE ECOWAS SINGLE CURRENCY
Ben Omar Ndiaye

Ndaye stressed that economic and monetary integration in Africa is considered an imperative for both promoting development and coping more effectively with external shocks entailed by globalisation. It is in this context that the ECOWAS member countries have decided to work for the creation of a common currency. His presentation comprised three parts: the analytical framework of the monetary integration process; the ECOWAS Monetary Cooperation Program (EMCP); and the road map to the creation of the single currency.

The process of monetary integration can be viewed in the context of the theory of optimum currency areas developed by Robert Mundell in the 1960s. A monetary zone has the following characteristics: the exchange rate between the currencies is fixed; currencies are convertible between themselves; foreign exchange reserves are centralised; and there is a common central bank and common economic policy bodies. Vis-à-vis third countries, there are floating exchange rates.

There are several costs and benefits of an integrated monetary zone. The costs would include abandoning the use of the exchange rate in the case of exogenous shocks; the loss of autonomy of the monetary policy and even fiscal policy. On the other hand, benefits include the end of speculation on the exchange rate, the elimination of cost of managing external resources and improving the cash value of the currency.

It is useful to compare the compliance of the ECOWAS monetary integration with the theory of optimum currency areas, including the degree of macroeconomic convergence. Significant efforts have been made to promote the free movement of people and goods, although there are still some barriers to the movement of goods mainly due to poor infrastructure. As for the degree of openness of the economies of the community, I estimate it to be about 55 per cent, while intra-community trade constitutes about 10 per cent of total trade. However, official statistics do not take into account the informal trade that is becoming increasingly significant.

Financial integration is a major weakness of ECOWAS. There is no harmonisation of fiscal policies at the state level and there are no money and capital markets across the community. Most countries export primary goods and have poorly diversified economies. Inflation rates in the area differ between countries of the franc zone and those outside it. However, the variability of these currencies remains low, with the exception of Liberia and Guinea.

Yet, these technical problems cannot be serious obstacles to the progress toward the single currency. The main obstacle – as we can clearly guess – is the lack of political will to implement the agreements signed by the leaders of ECOWAS.

Legal and regulatory instruments are in place, but the compliance required for macroeconomic and financial convergence is lacking and is delaying the process of monetary integration. For example, during the period 2000–2010, several countries were unable to meet the convergence criteria on budget deficit relative to GDP, inflation rate or rates of gross foreign exchange reserves (at least 6 months of imports). However, almost all countries seem to have met the criterion of budget deficit financing by the central bank to avoid using printing of money that generates inflation.

The experience of the eurozone is instructive. Studies have shown that this zone does not meet the criteria for an optimum currency area. Rather, it is founded on economic and financial criteria on the one hand, and political criteria, on the other hand. The WAEMU does not meet the criteria for an optimum currency area either, but experience shows that the adoption of a common currency promotes compliance with certain convergence criteria, such as inflation or budget deficits ceilings. No group of countries fulfils all the criteria set by the theory of optimum currency areas. And ECOWAS is far from fulfilling these criteria, as shown in the weak macroeconomic convergence.

In respect of the ECOWAS Monetary Cooperation Programme, the harmonisation of monetary and financial policies and payments is considered a crucial step in the implementation of the ECOWAS Treaty. But the existence of eight different, non-convertible currencies is a major obstacle to achieving this goal. To overcome it, monetary cooperation has been established through the WACH and the ECOWAS Multilateral Clearing Mechanism. These two mechanisms should help countries to use their own currencies in intra-community transactions, allowing them to save foreign exchange. They should also help simplify the settlement of commercial transactions through a multilateral clearing system.

Problems with monetary cooperation have arisen after and contributed to crippling the system. This led leaders to transform WACH into the West African Monetary Agency (WAMA) as far back as 1996. In addition to performing the functions of the ex-WACH, WAMA aims to: promote monetary cooperation of ECOWAS member countries; assist states in harmonising and coordinating their monetary and budgetary policies; provide monitoring and coordination of the monetary cooperation policy; and conduct studies to facilitate economic and monetary integration in ECOWAS. In this context, it was proposed in 1999/2000 to enlarge macroeconomic convergence criteria from four primary criteria to 10, including six secondary criteria. At the same time, member countries outside the CFA zone considered creating the West Africa Monetary Zone (WAMZ) in the framework of the fast-track initiative. In 2001, the ECOWAS Multilateral Surveillance Mechanism was created. But the deadlines were postponed several times. The WAMZ has not yet emerged, with a new deadline for 2015. The delay in its implementation in turn delayed the adoption of the single currency, now scheduled for 2020.

In light of these delays, a new approach was adopted in 2008, which includes three options: 1) The 'big bang' approach, which is based on a political decision of leaders; 2) The phased approach, based on the prior compliance with the prescribed eligibility criteria; and 3) the critical mass approach, meaning that countries representing at least 60 per cent of the community's GDP must meet the primary convergence criteria. The review of these three options led the convergence council to ask the ECOWAS Commission to conduct a feasibility study to determine the best option to achieve the single currency. In this context, a 2010–2020 roadmap was adopted, with specific objectives defined.

In conclusion, progress has been made in many areas, but there is still quite a way to go in order to reach the single currency. I am convinced that the benefits of the single currency are greater than the resulting costs. The ECOWAS countries have great interest in adopting a single currency in order to stimulate dynamic development in the community.

THE FIRST STEPS TO CREATING THE NILO – A NEW CURRENCY FOR AFRICA – **Yash Tandon**

Tandon argued that 'there is no country or region in the world that can enjoy real independence without owning and controlling its own money'. Money is a weapon of war par excellence. Economics is politics by other means. The empire uses economic tools to advance its strategic, political and economic interests around the world, especially to the detriment of weaker countries. Therefore, lack of control over one's currency ensures lack of control of one's economy and development policies.

The period of the generalised Fourth World War has started. What happened in Iraq and Libya, what is happening in Syria and the general situation in the Mediterranean, clearly illustrate this. Money is used by the US and its allies to play a destructive role against Iran in order to destabilise and destroy its currency and economy. Currency wars could keep this Fourth World War going for 50 years or more and drive Africans and Arabs into killing one another for years.

This is why Africa should have control over its own currency for political and strategic reasons. It would advance the cause of Pan-Africanism and enable countries of the continent to speak more effectively and with one voice in the global fora. Moreover, a single currency would guarantee Africa's security and political independence in this globalised and very uncertain world.

An African currency, which I call the nilo, should be a non-convertible currency and the conditions for its success include the following steps:

- Learning from the experience of other developing countries' in Latin America and Asia

- Overcoming barriers between African countries and moving toward a Customs Union,

- Creating a regional monetary agreement with regulations for the exchange rate and a Regional Bank, funded by countries on the continent

- Putting an end to the practices by which the savings of the African populations are exported to the West

- Reviewing all cooperation agreements and bilateral treaties that are dangerous instruments against Africa's fundamental interests and obstacles to its development

- Imposing an embargo on Economic Partnership Agreements (EPAs) and negotiate on Africa's own terms

- Linking the Bolivarian Alternative for the Americas (ALBA) with Africa

- Delinking from the global system in order for Africa to control its external relations

- Creating a firewall against speculative capital flows by instituting capital controls

- Mobilising African institutions to work closely together and speak with one voice in the international arena on behalf of African people.

COMMENTS BY DISCUSSANTS

Lansana Keita

I agree wholeheartedly with the analysis and proposals made by Yash Tandon. It is a fact, no country can be independent if it does not control its own currency, because issuing a currency is part of a country's sovereignty. Therefore, a country without its own currency cannot win the battle for development. Consider that 34 out of 54 African countries are ranked in the group of the poorest countries in the world by the United Nations and multilateral institutions. The reasons for this include, among others, the colonial legacy, the control of Africa's resources by former colonial powers, the lack of vision of African leaders and the influence of a neoliberal paradigm as illustrated by structural adjustment policies imposed by the IMF and the World Bank. The franc zone symbolises this control.

So, why does Africa continue to alienate its sovereignty by allowing foreign powers to control its currency? One explanation is the use of the African petty bourgeoisie, by the colonial powers as an instrument to subjugate other Africans. This class prefers consuming what is not produced in Africa. The middle classes do not have sufficient economic power but are benefiting from the system, which amounts to collective suicide.

We must do away with the narrow nationalism of African countries in order to move decisively toward regional and continental integration which would provide the conditions for genuine development. Then, he urged intellectuals to engage with people to lead the fight not only for monetary sovereignty, but also the sovereignty, independence and unity of Africa; a fight much valued by the fathers of Pan-Africanism, such as Kwame Nkrumah, and by revolutionary intellectuals such as Amilcar Cabral, Frantz Fanon and Cheikh Anta Diop.

Nicolas Agbohou

African member countries should not wait until 2020 to move to a single currency, because the CFA is scientifically organised genocide against Africa. Africa must create its own currency to control its own destiny. For example, the Chinese currency – the Yuan – is an instrument to bring out the creative genius of the Chinese people to work and create miracles. As long as Africa continues to wallow in beggary, it will remain in programmed bondage. This is evidenced by the condescension, arrogance and even contempt with which western countries are treating African countries and their 'leaders'.

Conclusion

Several other participants took the floor to make contributions. After the general debate, the following conclusions were reached:

♦ A currency fits into the triangle of sovereignty, security and development.

♦ The CFA is a system in which African countries are trapped, because when one does not control one's external relations, one has no way out. So, African countries should put an end to the Franc Zone and create their own monetary system. To this end, they should:

♦ Establish some budgetary discipline to prevent excesses

♦ Establish a foreign exchange control, because our borders are porous

♦ Completely reorganise the banking system

♦ Change consumption habits and consume what is produced and processed locally rather than what is imported

♦ Impose high taxes on luxury goods that are sources of outflows of foreign exchange

♦ Have a new type of leadership with a Pan-Africanist vision

♦ Engage more committed stakeholders in the struggle for the single African currency to pressure governments

♦ Link the single currency to a fairly high level of intra-African trade

♦ Embrace a process of deep decolonisation, especially in the minds of leadership

♦ The rate of indebtedness should not exceed the level of GDP growth

♦ African countries should learn from historical examples. One of such example is the 13 colonies that gave up their sovereignty and came together against Britain during the War of Independence, which gave birth to the United States. The 13 colonies' central banks established the Federal Reserve System in 1912 to serve their economies.

♦ Africa should also meditate on the example of the Chinese currency which is a non-convertible currency despite China being a strong nation, and in spite of pressures from the United States and western countries to make the yuan convertible.

PLENARY THREE

CONCLUSIONS AND RECOMMENDATIONS

Demba Moussa Dembele (ARCADE) and Carlos Cardoso (CODESRIA) presented the main conclusions and recommendations that came out of the discussions during the two days:

♦ It has been established that the CFA franc is not a currency for the development of African countries. It is part of the system set up by France to perpetuate its domination over these countries. It symbolises the continuation of the colonial pact. Therefore, the franc zone must be dismantled and replaced by a sovereign monetary system that meets the development needs of African countries.

♦ Participants commend the efforts being made to create a sub-regional currency in West Africa within the framework of ECOWAS. Participants support the creation of sovereign institutions of economic, monetary and financial governance to lay the foundations for the advent of a continental currency.

♦ Africa must learn from history as well as from other regions of the South, especially from the experiences of Latin America. In this regard, it is proposed to develop solidarity and exchanges between Africa and Latin America, particularly with the group of the Bolivarian Alternative for the Americas (ALBA). The African member countries of the CFA should also learn from the good practices and lessons from past and ongoing monetary experiences in other parts of Africa.

♦ The conclusions and recommendations of this conference should be disseminated at the highest level in Senegal, in other CFA countries and elsewhere in Africa in order to strengthen the political struggle to pressure leaders and policymakers to rethink the development of the continent.

♦ The conference is part of the political and citizen struggle that African intellectuals must lead for the end of the franc zone and of all systems of financial and economic domination of African countries. However, the fight should also be led by social movements and the general public, because it is the cause of all peoples of Africa. It may take a mass movement to convince leaders and policymakers to rethink their development policies

♦ ARCADE and CODESRIA pledge to publish a report of the conference proceedings in French and English.

♦ The findings of existing studies should be prepared in the form of policy briefs and sent massively to the offices of presidents and parliamentarians.

♦ Training sessions and workshops should be organised with parliamentarians and policy-makers on the issue of the currency. This would help challenge MPs and heads of state on the monetary and other development issues of the continent.

♦ A high-level conference should be organised on political dialogue between academics, researchers, representatives of social movements, policymakers, MPs and heads of state within one or two years under the auspices of CODESRIA and its partners.

♦ Africans must believe in themselves to take up the challenges facing their continent. As the martyr Steve Biko once said 'the most potent weapon in the hands of the oppressor is the mind of the oppressed'. Therefore, Africans must decolonise their minds, think for themselves and take their destiny into their own hands

MEETING WITH STUDENTS AT CHEIKH ANTA DIOP UNIVERSITY

Moderator:
Demba Moussa Dembele, President, ARCADE

The organisers of the conference – ARCADE and CODESRIA – proposed a discussion on the CFA franc at the Cheikh Anta Diop University. Together with a group of African students from the Centre Africain de Complémentarité Scolaire Universitaire et de Promotion (CACSUP), a public meeting was held on Saturday, 13 October. More than 500 students attended. The meeting hosted rich and lively debates between students and presenters, and the event was well covered by the broadcast and print media. To introduce the topic on the CFA franc, the floor was given to Nicolas Agbohou who, for more than 45 minutes held the audience spellbound with a presentation on all aspects of the CFA franc, from its origins to present day.

From 1945 to 1975 African countries deposited 100 per cent of their foreign exchange reserves in the transaction accounts in France; from 1975 to 2005, they deposited 65 per cent, and since 2005, 50 per cent of their reserves. France uses African reserves deposits to finance part of its budget deficit and to repay a portion of its debt. These deposits deprive African farmers of their income. Meanwhile, the amount of gold belonging to African countries in France is estimated at 300,000 tons.

Despite these injustices, attempts by African member countries to leave the CFA franc zone have been met with strong arm tactics from the colonial power, France. On 15 May 2011, the Ivorian authorities announced the creation of an Ivorian currency. This decision precipitated the fall of President Laurent Gbagbo, with French troops storming the presidential palace. Many people argue that the CFA franc is a strong currency and justify its fixed exchange rate with the euro, but this is a false debate. Take the Japanese yen for example. One euro is worth more than 100 yen, yet the Japanese currency is not weak at all.

More than 50 years after independence it is time to ask why West African countries are still under French tutelage? The answer lies primarily in the poor African leadership.

Following the expert presentations, many students spoke of their commitment to the struggle for the economic and monetary emancipation of Africa. The discussions highlighted the following:

♦ The inability or fear of leaders to tackle the problem of the CFA, because of coups and assassinations

♦ The need for greater public awareness about the currency issue

♦ International agreements imposed on African countries and that are against the fundamental interests of the African people

♦ Africa has all the wherewithal – natural resources and human expertise – to become an economic giant and hold its place in the world

♦ The only benefit of the CFA franc is bringing 15 African countries together

♦ Getting out of the franc zone is a prerequisite to propel the development of African member countries,

♦ A country without its own currency will be under perennial domination, because the creative genius of its people remains imprisoned. A country is not developed through begging.

Africa and the world are in a period of profound transformations in all areas, because of the current 'crisis of civilization' following the collapse of the dogmas and myths of the capitalist system. Around the world, deep challenges to the model imposed by the West are at work. New avenues are being explored that can lead to real development. Africa cannot afford to remain outside this trend. It must break with the legacy of colonisation and fundamentally rethink its development. The issue of the CFA franc falls within this context. Africans should adopt a policy based on endogenous values and the countries of the franc zone should have their own single currency that primarily takes into account the general domestic economic plan.

The meeting laid the foundation for a long-lasting cooperation between CACSUP and ARCADE, with an eye to promoting the campaign for monetary sovereignty among the student movement. In this regard, to create an African Network for Monetary Sovereignty (ANMS) was proposed and unanimously endorsed by the particpants. The ANMS should help educate the general public on the issue of currency and its significance in terms of national sovereignty and security. The network should undertake research, training, petitions and several other activities in order to keep the issue of sovereign currency high on the economic and political agenda in CFA countries and beyond.

Section 2

Papers

THE CFA FRANC A VECTOR OF MONETARY NAZISM
Nicolas Agbohou

The CFA franc (or Franc of the French colonies in Africa) was created by General Charles de Gaulle on 25 December 1945 under Article 3 of the Decree 45-0136. It was inspired by the monetary Nazism of Adolf Hitler, who invented and applied this principle effectively to all the European countries he invaded during the Second World War. The institutions of the CFA franc zone are the Conference of Heads of State, the Council of Ministers, three African Central Banks, and the National Credit Committees or Monetary Committees. These institutions, along with the principles of the franc zone are keeping African member countries in structural economic poverty. This will only be overcome when member countries achieve monetary sovereignty and begin generating wealth by processing all raw materials into finished products in Africa. Until such time, the franc zone policies will continue to hamper the development of all African countries that are trapped within its confines.

The Conference of Heads of State

The Conference of Heads of State is the supreme body of the franc zone. It decides on the accession of new members, and endorses the withdrawal and expulsion of members from the West African Economic and Monetary Union (WAEMU).

The Council of Ministers

The Council of Ministers 'provides the leadership of WAEMU, sets the monetary and credit policy of the union, provides the financing of economic activities and development of the member states, and determines the change in parity of WAEMU's currency'.[3] Several observations or critques have shown that the statutory powers of the Conference of Heads of State and the Council of Ministers are fictitious. For example, Côte d'Ivoire, under the rule of Laurent Gbagbo, was expelled in 2010 from the Central Bank of West African States (BCEAO) at the behest of France, without the prior favourable opinion of the Ivorian State, which could not vote for its own expulsion. Another illustrative case is that of Mali under Modibo Keita. After leaving the franc zone of their own accord on 1 July 1962, Mali led bitter and protracted negotiations with France to effectively re-join the franc zone in 1984. France also long opposed the membership of Guinea-Bissau in the franc zone. It was not until late 1996 that the country was admitted as a member of the CFA.

The monetary colonialism of France against Africa was openly revealed to unwary populations with the devaluation of the CFA franc in Dakar on 12 January 1994. According to Édouard Balladur, the prime minister of France at the time, this decision was taken unilaterally. Balladur noted that: 'The CFA franc was devalued in 1994 at the behest of France, because we felt this was the best way to help these countries towards their development.'[4] The status of African member countries was clear: they were subjected to the monetary whims of the coloniser and thus sovereignty and independence were severely restricted. Balladur rightly pointed out that: 'Currency is not a technical issue but a political one, which affects the sovereignty and independence of nations.'[5]

The CFA franc was wholly owned by France, and it changed parity according to the legitimate interests of the colonial power. African heads of state, including Omar Bongo, the former president of Gabon, who pointed out that 'nobody told us to

---

3 . Statutes of the BCEAO, Section 1, Title III, Article 38.
4 . Balladur, E. (1994) quoted in Jeune Afrique Economie 178, April.
5 . Balladur, E. (1990) quoted in Le Monde, 9 February. Read also in Géopolitique, No. 53, Spring 1996, p. 81.

devalue by 50% in LDCs[6], and 25% in MICs[7]. We were all put in the same basket'.[8]

Former Gabonese president, Etienne Gnassingbé Eyadema, went further to explain why, despite the general opposition by African heads of state, who were patronized and disempowered by France, the devaluation of the CFA franc took place under the eyes of the censor representing Michel Roussin, the then minister of cooperation: '... might is often right. I was not alone in making this warning, but France has decided otherwise. African voices did not count for much in this issue.'[9]

African Central Banks

The three African central banks are Central Bank of Comoros (BCC), the Bank of Central African States (BEAC) and the Central Bank of West African States (BCEAO). The BCC is the bank for the islands of the Islamic Federal Republic of the Comoros. Côte d'Ivoire, Togo, Benin, Burkina Faso, Mali, Niger, Senegal and Guinea Bissau are members of the BCEAO. The BEAC is the central bank of Gabon, Congo Brazzaville, Cameroon, Central African Republic, Chad and Equatorial Guinea. These three African central banks are managed by France, in a manner similar to the monetary Nazism suffered under occupation during the Second World War. Monetary Nazism was inspired by Hitler and manifested through the institutionalised presence of Nazis in the financial system in occupied countries. France is applying the same monetary Nazism in its former colonies through its omnipresence in the management of the three African central banks. For example, the African central banks are each administered by a board of directors. In the case of the BEAC, of its 13 directors, three represent the French Republic10; Two directors

---

6 . Least Developed Countries.
7 . Middle Income Countries.
8 . Omar Bongo, president of Gabon, interviewed by Jeune Afrique,1841, 17–23 April 1996, p. 38.
9 . Jeune Afrique, issue n° 1841, of 17-23 April 1996. p.38.
10 . Article 3 of the statutes of the BEAC.

of the 18 member board of the BCEAO are appointed by the government of France and they enjoy 'the same powers as the Directors appointed by the Members States of the Union'.[11] Of the eight directors of the BCC, 50 percent are from France and are appointed for four-year renewable terms.[12]

France also enjoys veto powers on the boards of all three African central banks. In the Comoros, decisions of the board 'are only valid if at least six of its members are present or represented. Deliberations must be adopted by at least five members present or represented.'[13] The board of directors of BEAC 'acts validly if at least one director from each Member State and one French Administrator are present or represented'.[14] When the agenda of a meeting of the board is of no interest to France, they only need to apply the empty chair policy to block the correct functioning of the central banks, and hence of their member states. The same French veto right is exercised at the BCEAO, which stipulates that changes in its own statutes inherited from the colonial era 'should unanimously be supported by members of the Board'.[15] This means that France continues to practice monetary colonialism through this legal provision, which is a powerful weapon for maintaining the status quo. Such monetary repression is particularly evident when it comes to the financing of economic activities of CFA member countries, because the central bank has the power to 'grant current account overdrafts, at its own discount rate, to the Treasuries of the States of the Union'.[16] Moreover, 'the Board of Directors determines the overall level of assistance which may be granted by the Central Bank to finance economic activity and development of each of the States of the Union.'[17]

---

11 . Article 10 of the Cooperation Agreement between France and WAEMU countries.
12 . Article 34, Title III the Monetary Cooperation Agreement between the French Republic and the Islamic Federal Republic of Comoros.
13 . Statutes of the BCC of Comoros, Title III, Article 38.
14 . Statutes of the Monetary Cooperation Convention between BEAC member countries and la France, Article 38.
15 . Statutes of the BCEAO, Article 51.
16 . Statutes of the BCEAO, Article 14.
17 . Statutes of the BCEAO, Article 52, par. 7.

By strictly controlling the monetary policies, France is crippling the economies of CFA member countries; undermining the labour force, and the inventive or creative genius of Africans; and deliberately keeping member countries in a state of an endless structural, socio-economic underdevelopment, which has negative consequences for the entire continent.

National Credit Committees

The control of national credit committees by Paris is part of the logic of impoverishment of the African states in the franc zone. The National Credit Committee 'is composed of the Minister of Finance, the two representatives of the State at the Board of Directors, four other members appointed by the Government of the State concerned and a representative of France'.[18] The allocation of the total amount of loans to member countries is operated by the National Credit Committees[19,20], the operating rules and tasks of which are defined by the board of directors. The latter has the power 'to revisit the decisions of the National Credit Committees which contravene the provisions of the statutes of the BCEAO and the general operating rules according to their jurisdiction as laid down by the Board of Directors'.[21]

As can be seen, France is present in all strategic decision-making spheres of the three African Central Banks. It controls Africans access to bank loans that are vital to economic development. This partly explains the very poor growth or even quasi-paralysis of the real purchasing power per capita (actual GDP/capita or PPP) over decades in some African countries of the franc zone, such as Côte d'Ivoire, Chad, Cameroon, the Central African Republic, Benin and Senegal, which in 1960 had a GDP higher than that of South Korea or China (see Table 1). Several decades

18 . Article 53 of the statutes of the BCEAO
19 . Also called National Monetary Committees in BEAC member countries
20 . Statutes of the BCEAO, Article 54
21 . Article 52 of the BCEAO, paragraph 6

later in 2010, the South Korean real GDP was $29,004. Despite the tripling of its population since 1950, China has become the second largest economy in the world. The Chinese GDP per capita was $7,599. In contrast to the Chinese and South Korean progress, nearly all the countries of the franc zone are becoming 'least developed countries' (LDCs), based on the ranking by the United Nations. According to the Human Development Index, the countries at the bottom of the scale are members of the franc zone, including Mali, Burkina Faso and Niger.

Table 1: Real GDP per capita or purchasing power parity of countries (1960–2010)

Countries	1960 (a)	1993 (a)	2010
South Korea	690	9 710	29 004
China	723	2 330	7 599
France	***	19 140	33 810
African countries in the CFA			
Cameroon	736	2 220	2 294
Chad	785	690	1 301
Central African Republic	806	1 050	758
Cote d'Ivoire	1 021	1 620	1 702
Congo Brazzaville	1 092	2 750	4 245
Benin	1 075	1 650	
Senegal	1 136	1 710	1 817
Gabon	1 373	3 861	15 054
Niger	604	790	690
Togo	411	1 020	851
Mali	541	530	1 186
Burkina Faso	290	780	1 187

Sources: a) - UNDP, 1996 Report and b) - The World Bank

The structural blockage, and the economic and financial plundering of the African countries is also driven by principles of the franc zone: 1) centralised exchange; 2) fixed parity between the CFA franc and the euro; 3) the free convertibility of CFA francs into Euros; and 4) the free movement of capital from the CFA franc zone to France. These principles are inspired by monetary Nazism and are fundamental barriers to real socio-economic growth of in CFA member countries. For example, France requires each African central bank to open and supply a current account with the French treasury, called the transaction account, which is fashioned after the Nazi model. As it invaded countries across Europe, Nazi Germany forced these countries to provide all the goods they needed. In return, the Germans opened bank accounts in Berlin for each occupied state. European vassal states exporting to Germany could only use their assets in Berlin with permission and were required to import all products from Germany. This commercial cooperation was termed the clearing mechanism and is explained below by the Pierre Carthala, a former minister of economy and finance:

> "Under an agreement reached in 1940, France finances exports to Germany. That means that every time a French factory works on behalf of Germany, it becomes a creditor of the German State to which it supplies, but in fact it is the French Treasury that provides the necessary advances in French francs. We are bearing the charges of industrial or commercial exports to Germany. In return we have a claim in Germany in Deutsche marks. We cannot get this credit apart from payments to be effected to Germany, hence, making it additional burdens for our cash. In 1943, advances for the clearing had reached alarming proportions. While in the course of previous years, payments amounted to two or three billion per month, in September 1943 however, advances have reached 7 billion per month. Advances made since October 1940 amounted to a total sum of 115 billion;

you can count that in 1943, the French Treasury will therefore bear an additional charge of 60 billion.[22]

In reality, Germany never paid supplier or creditor countries under its tutelage, reducing them to a pool of free labour:

> The establishment and functioning of the so-called compensation agreement earned considerable advantages to Germany. Thanks to this, they could buy for free and without limitation, all French resources they needed to continue the war and provide for the livelihood of their people.[23]

Hemmen, the former Plenipotentiary Ambassador of Germany to Paris, said that of all European countries, France was most afflicted by the systematic looting of monetary Nazism:

> The efforts already reported to save wherever possible the funds of the occupancy costs by channelling in all arguable cases through the clearing mechanism all German payment obligations relating to French supplies were continued until full depletion of any possibility. Thus, for consistency, the French government had to withdraw from its budget the amounts needed for its payments (...). In other words, the French government had – and to a growing extent – to finance itself our weapons and cantonment spending, our purchases of goods in France, as well as providing for French workers in Germany (...). The economic contribution of France to food and weapons for Germany was such that out of the total debt of Germany through the clearing mechanism toward 29 countries, to the tune of 20 million Marks, the portion relating to France was 8 and a half billion, representing 43%.[24]

22 . Cathala, P. (1948) Face aux réalités, la direction des finances françaises sous l'occupation, Ed. Du Triolet, p.35–36.
23 . Arnoult, P. (1951) 'Les finances de la France et l'occupation allemande (1940-1944). Ed. Puf, p.192.
24 . Hemmen, quoted by Arnoult, op.cit.

This same clearing system is duplicated in the transaction accounts model imposed by France on countries in neo-colonised Africa. The convention between France and the franc zone in Africa stipulates that:

> Member States agree to put together their foreign assets in a foreign reserve Fund. These reserves will be deposited with the French Treasury, in a current account called transaction account". [25] And the bank shall deposit into the transaction account the liquid assets it may earn outside its issuance area. [26]

Until 1973, African central banks were required to deposit to the transaction account all the foreign assets they held. The 1973 Convention, which introduced more flexible terms, states that African countries of the franc zone (African franc zone countries) must deposit at least 65 per cent of their foreign exchange reserves or export earnings with the French Treasury. In 2005, the amount was dropped to 50 per cent. In consideration for the strict observance of these principles, the French Treasury commits to provide all sums that the African Central Banks may need, for both local requirements and external payments in foreign currencies. [27] 'The transaction account may become debtor without any limitations assigned to the overdraft. When the balance is a debtor balance, the French Treasury receives some interests.'[28] paid by Africans. In other words, when the balance of the transactions account is in credit, the treasury pays interest to the African member states.

The French guarantee of convertibility of CFA francs into French francs in the past, and now into Euros, is a illusion. According to France's former minister of finance, Christine Lagard:

---

25 . Article 11 of the Monetary Cooperation Covenant between France and the BEAC member countries, 13 March 1973.
26 . Article 2 of the Transaction Account Covenant between France and the Franc Zone African countries (PAZF).
27 . Institut Technique de Banque, 'La Zone franc', 3rd edition, p. 15.
28 . Ibid.

The Bank of Central African States deposits, for example, about 90% of its assets with the French Treasury. If the leaders of the Central Bank are doing so, this means that they have some interest in it and that the deal is not that bad.[29]

Yet, the transaction accounts have very harmful consequences for Africans. According to Jean Boissonnat, a member of the Monetary Board of the Central Bank of France, France has enjoyed free access to African raw materials, much like the Nazi's did during the occupation of France. 'The franc zone,' Boissonnat wrote, 'has allowed France to be supplied with certain raw materials (lead, zinc, manganese, nickel, timber, phosphates, oilseeds, uranium...) without paying some currencies....' (Boissonnat 1960).

This represented a savings of $250 million a year in foreign currencies. It was estimated that 500,000 French citizens in the metropolitan France get their livelihoods from the franc zone economic bloc."[30] These free purchases of African raw materials by France are perpetuated by the leonine defense agreements and the 1963 Yaoundé I Convention, renewed in 1969 before transforming into Lomé I, Lomé II, Lomé III, Lomé IV and then Cotonou agreements, which later became the EPAs (Economic Partnership Agreements). All these defence agreements have a common denominator, which is to encourage African signatory countries to keep obediently supplying raw materials to France for free or at derisory prices. France, in compensation, credits the transaction accounts of its African suppliers with the Treasury in Paris. So, with simple plus (+) signs with no foreign currency expense, France is methodically and industriously plundering the many treasures of its African suppliers under its tutelage.

---

29 . Christine Lagarde, idem

30 . Boissonnat, J. (1960) 'La Zone Franc: Survivance du Passé ou Promesse d'Avenir', La Croix, 17 February.

For the record, when importing commodities from Ghana, Nigeria, Peru or any other non-CFA franc zone country, France disburses foreign currencies to pay, unlike from the CFA franc zone countries that are victims of their multifaceted, neo-colonial cooperation agreements essentially beneficial to France alone. Indeed, France and Europe are very poor in raw material, according to Edgard Pisani, a former EEC commissioner for cooperation and development:

> "Let us be clear: Europe has little mineral resources. Its subsoil is poor, because it was overexploited. Its dependence is huge, economically dangerous, strategically threatening... The subsoil of Africa, the Caribbean, the Pacific (the resources of the seabed) is rich but not much known and exploited. The general conditions (political, economic and technical) in these countries are discouraging private investors. It is of mutual interest that the exploitation is launched taking into consideration the legitimate needs of each partner: security of supply for Europe, value addition of natural resources in ACP countries... Therefore, Europeans should stop believing they are the generous, helping donor". [31]

To bridge the deficit and meet its raw material requirements, and building on the lessons of the monetary Nazism, France signed, in 1961, defence agreements that gave it ownership of the natural resources of its African partners. More specifically, under Article 3 of the France-Africa Defence Agreement, the African countries involved: 'shall inform the French Republic of the policy they have set in regard to strategic raw materials and commodities and the measures that they are proposing to implement such policy. With regard to those materials and commodities, the African signatories of this agreement for Defense purposes, shall sell in priority to the French Republic (...) and get their supplies in priority from the same.'[32]

---

31. Pisani, E. (1984) in Laffont, R. (ed) La main et l'outil, Paris, p. 247
32. Annex II of the France-Africa defence cooperation Agreements, signed in Paris on 24 April 1961

Jean Foyer, the minister for cooperation under De Gaulle, commented ironically that this defence agreement served to better enlighten some Africans who were still unaware of the objective realities of French colonialism against Africa: 'We have signed agreements with Africans called agreements on strategic raw materials that simply obliged them to provide us in the first place, to grant us concessions.'[33]

Many acknowledge unequivocally that the transaction accounts are for the benefit of France. For example, the economist Bruno Coquet wrote:

> "The costs of ensuring convertibility of the currencies of the area proved quite low from the perspective of France... At the beginning of its existence, the franc zone has played a significant role in providing foreign currencies to France. In 1969, the positive balance of transaction accounts reached 8.9% of the foreign exchange reserves of France."[34]

African capital is used to cover budget deficit and repay debt of France. Author Xavier de la Fournière recalls that:

> "The advantage of having credit balances in transaction accounts for the French Treasury is real, because they are one of the resources used by the French Treasury to finance the burden resulting from the outstanding part of the enforcement of the Finance Act and the public debt amortization."[35]

African capital alleviates French balance of payment deficits. The Jenneney Report (1963) noted:

---

33 . Jean Foyer, Minister for Cooperation, 1960-1962. See Le Roy, G. and Osouf, V. (2007) Cameroun, Autopsie d'une independance.
34 . Coquet, B. and Daniel J.M. (1992) 'Quel avenir pour la zone franc cfa?' Observatoires et diagnostics économiques, No. 41, July, p. 241.
35 . De la Fournière, X. (1971) La zone Franc, P.U.F. No. 868.

When the countries of the franc zone export more than they import, they provide France with currencies. These are useful if at the same time its own balance of foreign payments is in deficit.[36]

The former president of Gabon, Omar Bongo, put it bluntly:

> We are in the franc zone. Our transaction accounts are managed by the Bank of France in Paris. Who benefits from the interests generated by the interests of our money? – France does.[37]

As a member of the Board of Directors of the three African central banks where it has a veto, France uses the profits made by these three currency issuing institutions. For example, in 2005 France took a bond loan worth around CFA900 billion. The statement of accounts of BCEAO as at 31 December 2005 showed that 'the currency portfolio consists mainly of bonds acquired and mainly comprised of government bonds issued by France (888.9 billion).'[38]

France issues securities called bonds, which BCEAO buys unwillingly instead of investing that money for the development of African member countries of the franc zone. This devious method is consequently depriving African countries of the money they badly need to eradicate the structural poverty. Thus, Africans are giving their common permanent executioner some powerful weapons and actively contributing to their own economic enslavement.

For example, in 2007, out of a total of CFA6,000 billion, the BEAC contributed more than CFA4,000 billion to the French treasury and only injected CFA2,000 billion into the economy of the member countries: In 2007, BEAC made payments

---

36 . Commission of Study of the Policy of Cooperation with the Developing Countries: Jeanneney Report (1963) 'La politique de coopération avec les pays en voie de développement', Paris, Documentation Française.
37 . Omar Bongo, interviewed by Libération, Paris, 18 September, 1996. p. 6.
38 . Ibid.

to 'the Transaction Accounts to the tune of 4,311.7 billion CFA francs at the end of March 2007'[39] compared to the 'loans to the economy established at 2,055.9 billion FCFA as at 31 March 2007...'[40]

The use of the CFA franc is imposing an endless monetary and fiscal discipline on Africans. The Managing Director of IMF clearly stated that:

> "pegging African currencies to a hard currency – the Euro – implies that tight monetary policies should be pursued by African central banks... The statutes of (African) central banks in the area include rules that institutionalize monetary discipline without which the franc zone could not exist... The conservation of parity and the fixity of African currencies exchange rates with the franc in the past, and now with the Euro require public finance stabilization policies to be pursued in most countries despite the difficulties noted".[41]

The fiscal and monetary discipline imposed in the franc zone manifests in the following, among other realities:

♦ Inadequate spending on national education, health, housing, agriculture, national defence, transportation, etc. The State gives up its regulatory functions by wrongly hiding under the veil of the global, economic neoliberalism, which is inhumane and inappropriate to the realities of African countries.

♦ The rise in interest rates to reduce bank lending to businesspeople and to strengthen the CFA franc pegged to the strong Euro.

---

39 . Monetary situation of CEMAC as at 31 March 2007.
40.. Ibid.
41 . Speech by M. Jacques de LAROSIERE at the meeting of Ministers of the franc zone - Thursday 17 September 1992. Theme of the meeting: the future of the franc zone in the economic and monetary union. Consulting the Bank of France – Directorate General for Foreign Services. Franc Zone Department. No. 92- 489, p. 8.

+ The growth in the level of tax pressure to increase government revenue, while reducing the already skeletal purchasing power of the average citizens who are getting even poorer.

This supports the observation that monetary bondage leads to subjugation and underdevelopment. This is also apparent in the agricultural sectors of CFA member countries. The average African farmer earns CFA100,000 per year, much of which is stored in France, depriving farmers and other citizens of their rightful revenue. The cleverly programmed summary execution of these 100 million African farmers and at the expense of funding the development of the economies of the African continent is nothing but an organized human tragedy with a whiff of disguised racism.

Transaction accounts require Africans to also deposit their gold stocks in the Bank of France to support the CFA franc. For example, the African gold stock of BCEAO held by the Central Bank of France as at 31 December 2001 was estimated at CFA206,528 billion. Thanks to the contributions of Africans, France is today one of three countries in the world with over 3,000 tons of gold in store.

Transaction accounts are a way for France to discipline African leaders. More than half of the public finances of African states are in exile in the hands of the former. African heads of state who challenge this neo-colonial monetary order are disciplined, removed from power and in some cases killed. Several examples are pertinent here: The president of Togo, Sylvanus Olympio was assassinated on January 13, 1963, just two days before his government was to introduce a new currency. After coining a local currency in 1962, Malian president Modibo Keita was forced to return to the franc zone before being removed from power and thrown into prison, where he was poisoned. Presidents Ousmane of Niger, and Patassé of Central African Republic lost power when they challenged the attempts by the IMF to dictate financial legislation. Perhaps the most expressive case of disciplining African leaders is that of Ivorian President Laurent Gbagbo ousted on 11 April 2011. From 11 February 2011, upon instruction by France, and through order by BCEAO all the subsidiaries of French banks in Côte d'Ivoire closed without notice. These include BICICI, which is a subsidiary of BNP Paribas and SGBCI the subsidiary of Societe Generale. Other local commercial banks followed the move. They were then nationalised and re-opened in the interest of employees, investors, the national economy and the political system of Gbagbo whose finance minister noted:

> The net banking income of these banks is made up of more than 55 % of the costs of keeping accounts and other bank charges levied on the accounts of civil servants. The rest comes from coffee and cocoa export transactions. We mainly discovered why these banks do not want to give credit to companies. They have some net resources guaranteed by the salaries of public officials... The French banks in Côte d'Ivoire are providing interbank funding to other countries in the sub-region; in other terms, the Ivorian subsidiaries are financing the common charges of the African subsidiaries of those banks... BICICI made a deposit of more than 30 billion CFA francs, representing nearly 45 million Euros in the accounts of BNP Paribas at a preferential rate. In other words, BICICI has immobilized that sum outside the financial system and outside the African banking system. Despite the injunctions of the Banking Commission, BICICI has never returned this astronomical amount to its accounts.[42]

This provides further indication that the mission of the franc zone is to further enrich France to the detriment of African member countries. Indeed, Katina noted the intent of the Sarkozy and the government of France in respect of the attacks on Côte d'Ivoire:

---

42. Minister Kone Katina, quoted in Onana, C. (2011) 'Cote d'Ivoire, Le coup d'Etat', Edition Duboiris, pp. 310–312

> "Actually, France under the rule of Sarkozy would have lost the war against Cote-d'Ivoire had the date of March 31, 2011 elapsed, since the creation of the national currency – the notes of which were already drawn and the company already known – was planned for May 15, 2011 at the latest. Economically, the government beat France in the banking confrontation the latter had waged. Furious to see its failure, France waged the militarily confrontation."[43]

For daring to create his own currency, President Gbagbo was called to order in a military manner by Sarkozy, who wrote the following to the president GoodLuck Jonathan:

> "The political situation in Cote-d'Ivoire is deteriorating every day... France will play its part in restoring the rule of law and especially using all legal avenues to obtain the departure of the outgoing President Laurent Gbagbo... You must send a clear message to Mr Laurent Gbagbo telling him that military forces will dislodge him. Our forces based in Côte d'Ivoire will take part in the operation... It would be disastrous for democracy in Africa to let such an affront of outgoing President Laurent Gbagbo to stay in power. Power sharing is unacceptable. The only political solution is the unconditional departure of Laurent Gbagbo who continues to usurp a power which he is no longer entitled to."[44]

Thus, the fallacious argumentation of democracy is used to conceal the real reason that prompted Sarkozy to violently remove his Ivorian counterpart: the Ivorian currency that was to be issued to the detriment of the CFA franc.

---

43 . Ibid.
44 . Ibid.

Fixed parity between CFA franc and Euro

The CFA franc being pegged to the Euro is disadvantageous to Africans for several reasons: The overvaluation of the CFA franc makes African economies less competitive. Thus, African countries are losing significant portions of their foreign markets to global competitors. Africans also lose a lot of money when their export earnings are converted into Euros. This means that if, for example, the Euro is double the US dollar, the export revenues of Africans are reduced automatically by half. According to Franck Merceron, Director of the Swiss NGO Helvetas, which supports a program of organic and fair trade cotton in Africa, the rise in the Euro and consequent overvaluation of the CFA means: 'We are losing 40% of the price to the exchange rate.'[45]

Programmed devaluation of the CFA franc

During the era of Nazi occupation, the Germans devalued the local currency of occupied countries to increase their own purchasing power. In 1994, France applied the same method of devaluation to African CFA member countries to better exploit them peacefully. Today, devaluation of the CFA franc is undertaken for the reconstruction of the European Union with the free raw materials from Francophone Africa. Former prime minister Pierre Mesmer prophesied and advised that devaluation was par for the course, something that African states would have to accept, and warned that the guarantee of French sponsorship was a wild dream:

> Do not believe in Santa Claus. France alone in the European Union will not be able to fill in budget deficits of Africans for forever... Just like in 1993, the CFA franc will be overvalued in light of the economic, and especially financial, reality of African countries.[46]

---

45 . swissinfo.ch (2008) 'Le coton plus précieux que l'or', 2 January, http://www.swissinfo.ch/fre/le-coton–plus-pr%C3%A9cieux-que-l-or–2-2-/529840, accessed 5 July 2015
46 . Messmer, P. (1998) in Jeune Afrique No.1943, 7–13 April, p. 57.

It is impossible for Africans to manoeuvre the exchange rate in their favour. The fixed parity between the CFA franc and the Euro does not allow Africans to handle the exchange rate in a sovereign manner. For instance, by weakening their dollar, the Americans are performing monetary protectionism. The commodities of their European competitors become too expensive while theirs appear more competitive. Africans have rejected unwillingly this economic protection tool.

Moreover, the overvalued CFA franc does not promote trade between the countries of the franc zone and the rest of Africa, despite the continent potentially constitutes one of the world's largest markets. Currently the countries of the franc zone are excluding themselves from the intra-African market in favour of their subordinate economic integration into the European Union.

The principle of free convertibility of the CFA franc

This principle ensures for France the free, unlimited convertibility of CFA francs to Euros. This principle imposes severe limitations:

- The CFA franc is not a convertible currency.
- CFA Francs of the BCEAO and BEAC are not interchangable, This divides West Africa and Central Africa in commercial terms at a time when major economic and trading blocs are in place, such as NAFTA in North America, MERCOSUR in South America, ASEAN in Asia and the European Union. Thus, Africa is weakened by the fragmentation of the CFA franc.

France relies on the specious argument that it guarantees indefinitely the conversion of the CFA currency to justify its control over African central banks and thus keep Africans permanently underdeveloped. The French-African Monetary Cooperation states that 'the Bank of Central African States is an African multinational institution, in the management and control of which France is participating in return for the guarantee it provides to its currency.'[47] Yet, the French guarantee is not a driver in attracting foreign direct investment (FDI) into African countries of the franc zone. For example, in 2007, 'China and France signed commercial contracts on November 26 to the tune of 20 billion Euros.'[48], although the Chinese yuan is not convertible. Furthermore, France is the first country contributing FDI to Morocco, Tunisia and Algeria. In 2007, 'President Nicolas Sarkozy announced in Rabat that France had signed contracts with Morocco for an amount of €3 billion.'[49] These three Arab countries, namely Morocco, Tunisia and Algeria, have left the CFA franc respectively in 1957, 1958 and 1963 to issue their own national currencies with brilliant results that are visible and undeniable, while Africans in the franc zone remain notoriously poor, while supplying France with foreign currency.

All foreign currencies given to African countries in the CFA franc zone as grants, foreign loans, foreign direct investment and other forms of financial aid are actually received by France. France receives these monies and manufactures CFA franc notes for African countries. Thus, the colonial project is perpetuated through the CFA franc and the coloniser benefits from the principle of free transferability of capital.

The principle of free transfer of capital from the franc zone countries to France ensures the legal and continuous flight of the very capital needed to develop the countries concerned. Even former president François Mitterrand confessed that the drain contributes to the ruination of African economies:

> ...Africans are continuously robbed. They are constantly impoverished. There will be more capital flows from Africa to developed countries than the opposite. Huge sums are taken away on the back of Africa.[50]

47. Article 7 of the Convention of the Monetary Cooperation Convention between the BEAC member States and France, signed in Libreville (Gabon), on 13 March, 1973.
48. Agence France Presse (2007) 22 October.
49. Challenges Magazine (2007), 29 November.
50. François Mitterrand, quoted in Adler, L. (1995) L'année des adieux, Paris, édition Flammarion. Adler is a historian and journalist, former cultural advisor to Mitterrand, and cultural facilitator of 'cercle de minuit' on France 2, a public television station.

The free transfer of capital does not contribute to the formation of the national and continental savings that are required for endogenous financing of investments, and hence development. The virtual absence of national savings justifies the continued resort to external debt which mortgages the country's future. Under these conditions, it is difficult to promote the emergence of a business class that is able to sustain the national economy.

Conclusion

This brief analysis of the institutions and the principles of the franc zone exposes the major drawbacks of this currency, the rejection of which is paramount for all stakeholders who want to break with neocolonialism.

THE CFA FRANC AT THE CROSSROADS: REFORMING OR DISMANTLING? – SANOU MBAYE

The countries of the franc zone, which share a common currency (the CFA franc), are being left out of Africa's economic revival. Since 2000, countries of sub-Saharan Africa have experienced an average growth between 5 per cent and 7 per cent, which is double the growth of the countries of the franc zone.[51] Seven of the 10 economies with the highest growth in the world over the next five years will be in Africa, but none of the countries of the franc zone will be among them.[52] The reasons for this are twofold. The first is the monetary policy of both central banks of the franc zone, namely the Central Bank of West African States (BCEAO) and the Bank of Central African States (BEAC). The second reason is the lack of economic integration of the two communities of the franc zone – the Economic Community of West African States (WAEMU) and the Community of Central African States (CEMAC).

The policies of the central banks

The monetary policies of the central banks of the franc zone are founded on inflation-control strategy and on the exchange rate, convertibility and free transfer of the CFA franc. In terms of inflation-control strategy, the BCEAO and the BEAC have resorted to high lending interest rates to ensure price stability in the WAEMU and CEMAC. This restrictive credit policy stems from a poor assessment of the true causes of the price increases in the franc zone countries. The two central banks link price increases to excess money supply, which is false because price increases are more exogenous than endogenous. There are currently inflationary pressures,

---

51 . Roxburgh, C. et al (2010) 'Lions on the move: The progress and potential of African economies', McKinsey Global Institute (MGI), June. http://www.mckinsey.com/insights/africa/lions_on_the_move, accessed 15 July 2015.
52 . The Economist (2011), 'The lion kings?', 6 January, http://www.economist.com/node/17853324, accessed 15 July 2015.

but these are due to internal factors such as insufficient and unstable agricultural supply. Inflation is essentially of an imported origin, linked to increasing cost of oil and food. The high cost of money-lending in the franc zone can in no way alter these parametres. To provide a solution to the inadequacy and instability of agricultural supply, it would have been more logical to promote policies for easy access to low interest loans for producers in order to boost food production, and thus reduce and stabilise food prices.

The insistence of central banks to confine themselves to this anti-inflationary logic has made them neglect another important aspect of their mission, which is to promote economic growth in member countries. Abusing high interest rates as a tool for monetary control, the BCEAO has deliberately exacerbated the difficulties of access to credit for governments and business people to finance their activities.[53] It further restricted the leeway for states by eliminating the outstanding it used to lend them up to 20 per cent of the previous tax revenue, making them once again hostages of French loans and budgetary policies.

Only French businesses can thrive in such an environment thanks to the monopoly they enjoy in key sectors of the economy, to subsidies from France, to Coface guarantees, to the generosity of commercial banks and central banks in terms of discount and rediscount and through access to a protected market. As a custodian of a large portion of domestic savings and financial flows, a sanctuary of speculative capital induced by the liberalisation of exchange rate policies and in a situation of permanent excess liquidity, the French commercial banks are accumulating profits by granting short-term loans to states at usurious rates used to finance their imports for oil, foodstuffs, capital and consumer goods. Furthermore, the path followed by BCEAO and BEAC in setting interest rates contrasts sharply with that of other central banks. Faced with the slowdown of economic activity and the threat of recession that

---

53 . Nubukpo, K. (2007) 'Politique monétaire et servitude volontaire: la gestion du franc CFA par la BCEAO', Politique Africaine, No. 105, March, pp. 70–82.

the financial meltdown of 2008 and the euro crisis are posing to the world, they are advocating policies to reduce interest rates in order to facilitate business recovery.

The US Federal Reserve set its lending rate at 1 per cent after the September 2001 attacks. It has maintained this policy of credit relaxation and will do so at least until 2015. The European Central Bank, the Bank of England and the Bank of Japan are pursuing similar policies. So, logically, BCEAO should have done the same. Yet, in terms of exchange rate policy, the BCEAO pegs the exchange rate of the CFA franc to the euro through a fixed exchange rate, convertibility and free transfer of money. Since it was established in 1998, the European Central Bank (ECB) is practicing a strong euro policy to raise the ambitions of the euro to become an international reserve currency. But if the Europeans, whose intra-community trade amounts to 80 per cent can live with the appreciation of the euro with respect to the dollar, this is not the case for countries of the franc zone. Their intra-regional trade is limited and they remain dependent on imports of food, manufactured goods, and common consumer products. Exports – oil, coffee, cocoa, cotton, gold, uranium, etc. – are denominated in dollars. The appreciation of the CFA franc vis-à-vis the dollar wipes out the competitiveness of CFA members' export sectors, widens their deficits and increases their debts.

The choice of a high exchange rate of the CFA franc is another practice of central banks in the franc zone that differs from that of other central banks that engage in merciless currency wars to increase the competitiveness of their exports. Since 1 January 1994, the Central Bank of China has pegged its currency – the yuan – to the dollar at a very low exchange rate, which gives it a competitive advantage over its western competitors and increased export opportunities for manufactured goods. The Federal Reserve, the European Central Bank, the Bank of England and the Bank of Japan even resort to printing massive amounts of electronic money, which they pour on the foreign exchange market to lower the price of their currencies, or to fund economic revival programmes and to rescue banks at the risk of plunging the world into a vicious cycle of inflationary surges with unpredictable consequences. It is good to remember that in the 1930s, monetary disputes of a similar nature led to competitive devaluations and protectionism, and runaway inflation, which in turn led to economic disaster and the rise of Hitler and Nazi ideology in Germany, and then the Second World War.

The international environment of 'currency war' and the atrophy of the economies of the franc zone show the absurdity of claims of monetary orthodoxy by the central banks of the franc zone. Without lapsing into complacency, monetary policy should be expansionary and not restrictive.

The franc zone hinders development in African countries

Fixed parity with the euro, convertibility and free transfer of the CFA franc are guaranteed by France in return for the deposit by the member countries of part of their foreign exchange earnings to the French treasury. At the dawn of independence, the currency deposit required by France to cover the CFA franc supply was 100 per cent. It was reduced to 65 per cent in 1973 and has been capped at 50 per cent since September 2005.

The current foreign reserves of the franc zone countries are excessive. According to the Bank of France, the coverage rate of the CFA franc monetary emission exceeds 110 per cent, while it should be capped at no more than 20 per cent in compliance with relevant accepted international standards on the one hand, and with the agreements signed between France and the countries of the franc zone on the other hand. Yet, the general trend of central banks is to avoid excessive reserve accumulation due to the losses they entail. In the franc zone, the losses are incurred for several reasons: surplus reserves are not used to fund capital expenditure or repay a portion of the external debt and thus reduce interest payments; the cost of the yield differential between the two per cent remuneration offered by France and the highest cost of instruments in which the reserves could have been invested; and the cost of losses generated by the appreciation of the currency.

All the reserve policies of the BCEAO boil down to vast subterfuge, which feeds a fool's bargain. Guaranteeing a fixed parity for a strong CFA franc keeps the French firms immune to common currency depreciations. Convertibility and free transfer enable them to repatriate the profits they reap. At the same time, the countries of the franc zone are constantly resorting to aid from France to survive, while huge sums of foreign currencies earned through the labour of their populations are subtracted arbitrarily by France to finance their development.

Exploring another exchange policy

The countries of the franc zone are facing chronic structural deficits and serious payment difficulties. Their economic activities are mainly based on the production and export of commodities. At this early stage of their development, the logic should be that they adopt a foreign exchange policy based on the non-convertibility and non-transferability of the CFA franc, and a parity pegged to a pool of currencies at fluctuating and beneficial exchange rates. To do this, they must declare an exchange rate regime that gives them control over all foreign exchange transactions. This legal restriction would ensure the rigorous management of inflow and outflows of foreign exchange, which would in turn ensure allocation to key development sectors of the economy. This is the monetary policy enforced by African countries such as South Africa, Nigeria, Kenya, Ethiopia, Angola and Ghana, all of which are now ahead in terms of development. This is also the case for emerging countries such as China, India, Korea, Malaysia, Turkey and Brazil. The Chinese giant for example, does not allow the liberalisation of the foreign exchange market in order to avoid significant risks to economic growth by an uncontrolled outflow of foreign exchange. Its currency is not freely convertible or freely transferable. So, why would the CFA franc be?

With regard to economic integration, the countries of the franc zone suffer economic fragmentation along with intra-community trade being strangulated by tariffs. A huge paradox of the CFA franc is the fact that it is the common currency of countries that do not share a common market. To remedy this, the WAEMU Commission was created in 1994, following the devaluation of the CFA franc. The criteria to harmonise the economic integration policies of its members were copied from the European Maastricht Treaty and set out permitted levels for inflation, debt and budget deficits.

The difference in development between the countries of the European Union and the countries of the franc zone should have prompted the WAEMU to be more creative and pragmatic in selecting its own convergence criteria. For instance, instead of the basic budget deficit it could have only required the equilibrium of the current structural balance. In other words, to allow deficits in order to support economic activity and to lay the foundations for future growth, while devoting the indebtedness of states exclusively to financing public investment. The current difficulties facing the countries of the franc zone make compliance with the set criteria a delusion and the project for economic union remains a challenge, thus exacerbating structural imbalances.

What future for the CFA franc?

The CFA franc is at a crossroads. It was created in France by a decree signed by General de Gaulle on 25 December 1945 to rationalise the exploitation of French colonies in the regional federations of West and Central Africa. The abolition of the CFA franc should have followed the dismantling of the federal structure of French colonies after independence. Under the same circumstances, Britain abolished the West African pound, which was common colonial-era currency in Nigeria, Ghana, Sierra Leone and The Gambia. In view of the poor conditions that countries in the franc zone are trapped in after more than half a century of independence, the time to reform or abolish the CFA franc is now.

This would require a complete restructuring of the system and an entire review of the provisions governing the parity, free transferability and convertibility of the CFA franc. They must be replaced by a system of non-convertibility and non-transferability of the currency whose parity must be pegged to a basket of selected currencies and not just the euro. The protagonists to decide such a change are the countries of the franc zone, their populations, the BCEAO and France.

Member countries of the franc zone have never had a voice in the management of their money. Worse, their leaders and elites accommodate and benefit from the situation. Indeed, before taking leadership in government, a number of them held positions at the highest level of such institutions as BCEAO and West African Development Bank (BOAD), or in the French commercial banks. Not surprisingly, none of the current leaders of member countries of the franc zone appear to be interested in reform. It is the average citizens who suffer the consequences of such instransegence: poverty, unemployment, social unrest, insecurity, famine, strife and social conflict. And when this leads to wars, France sends troops to restore order and then submits the bill for collection through the withholding of the very funds that these countries have lodged with them.

In a context of free movement of capital and rigid peg to the euro, the BCEAO and BEAC are, in turn, unable to pursue an independent monetary policy adapted to the cycle of the WAEMU and CEMAC economies.[54] In its Monetary Policy Committee

---

54. Mundell, R.A. (1961) 'A theory of optimum currency areas', *American Economic Review*, 51(4), pp. 657–65.

(MPC), which is in charge of defining and conducting the monetary policy in respect of the franc zone, the representative of the French treasury has one vote while the president of the WAEMU only has an advisory role. The BCEAO declared its independence vis-à-vis the WAEMU but not vis-à-vis the French treasury, which acts as a sounding board and a tool for the domination of the community countries it purports to represent and serve.[55] The economies of the franc zone are thus controlled and unable to self-manage at national, regional or local levels..[56]

France has decisive political influence over its former African colonies, including veto power in the management of the BCEAO and the BEAC. So it can block any action it perceives as contrary to its interests. The question that arises is whether or not this system is actually profitable to them. Colonial relics and domination can undoubtedly lead to thinking so, but the facts are increasingly belying them.

The increasing presence in Africa of actors such as China, India, Korea, Malaysia, Turkey and Brazil has given African countries more export opportunities, as well as a new cooperation model based on trade, investment and technology transfer. This has broadened their options for economic growth and provided greater flexibility and significant opportunities to advance development. It is in this context of reshaping global and African relations that the euro crisis is taking place, causing the slowdown of economic activity in France and many countries of the euro zone, resulting in economic recession, debt crisis, austere fiscal stabilisation programmes, rising unemployment and social unrest.

It would follow that leaders of the franc zone and their French allies have an obvious opportunity to define a new framework for cooperation. However, neither the leaders

---

55 . See: Tchundjang Pouemi, J. (1979) 'Monnaie, servitude et liberté : la répression monétaire de l'Afrique', Editions Menaibuc, Yaoundé.
56 . Bayart, Jean-François (1999) 'L'Afrique dans le monde: une histoire d'extraversion', Critique Internationale, April, No. 5, pp. 97–120.

of the franc zone, nor the French seem able to start. The francophone African elites appear loathe to break away from the past and to forge a more independent role. As for the French, they are preserving the status quo by keeping the architecture of the franc zone and offering moralising sermons on the need to fight poverty, corruption and bad governance as if the failures in the franc zone are not linked to a failure of governance of those giving the lessons.

Analyses suggest that the impact of the European crisis in Africa will be particularly felt on official development assistance, the volume of which may decrease due to budgetary restrictions in countries affected by the euro crisis. Such a prospect should be an unexpected opportunity for Africa and the West, to heal their mutual addiction to aid. Productive investment and fair trade should be favoured in cooperation and development programmes, as evidenced by the success of the cooperation with the so-called new emerging countries with rapid and sustained industrial development. Ideally, public support should only play a role in bridging public and private investment in the form of concessional loans and funds to support agricultural prices, social programmes and peacekeeping forces.

Therefore, there is indeed a convergence of interests for win-win cooperation between the countries of the franc zone and France. The reform of the franc zone should be at the forefront of measures to be considered. It is time for leaders of CFA member countries to free themselves and speak in unison in order to maximise the benefits from cooperation with France in the current geopolitical environment. Similarly, France must realise that the development of its former colonies in Africa could serve its interests better than the status quo of systematic exploitation.

Leaders and monetary authorities of the franc zone, together with the French treasury and the IMF, must evaluate the benefits, disadvantages and needed reforms to the system and draw up frameworks for investment and credit policies and trade agreements. This is a prerequisite for the members states of the franc zone to recover their full monetary sovereignty, their ability to articulate exchange rate and viable development policies, and to find a solution to the social disruptions and the vicious cycle of violence that has so far characterised life in the CFA franc countries.

This will require a radical change in the attitudes of Africans and their French allies, as well as in the complex relationships of dependency and paternalism that is the legacy of a heavy colonial history. The economic environment prevailing in Africa and Europe is favourable to such changes and to a radical revisioning of current development strategies.

Conclusion

The status quo that the French leaders and their franc zone allies have always favoured is counter to peace and security and development in the region, as evidenced by the more frequent violent attacks in member countries of the franc zone. Sooner or later, they will lead to the dismantling of the system with all the chaos that the collapse of a currency area entails. An agreement must be reached to determine the allocation of assets, liabilities and community reserves, and each country should coin its own currency and reserve the right to join the project of a regional monetary union within ECOWAS. It would be useful to learn from past and present experiences of monetary unions, including those of Europe and the franc zone, to avoid cutting corners in the process. Monetary union should ideally be preceded by political union if it is to survive and yield all the expected positive effects.

First and foremost the focus should be on the creation of a single market that runs smoothly. The idea that a common currency comes first and is a short-cut to integration can be misleading and complex. Let us remember that Bismarck began first by establishing the customs union of the German Lander before unification and that the US existed prior to the creation of the dollar.

THE FRANC ZONE: AN INSTRUMENT FOR DEVELOPMENT OR TOOL OF DOMINATION?

Demba Moussa Dembele

Introduction

The controversy over the CFA franc is not new. Recall the famous book by Joseph Tchundjang Pouémi (1981), Monnaie, servitude et liberté: la répression monétaire de l'Afrique (Money, bondage and freedom: monetary repression on Africa). His death under suspicious circumstances led to speculation about assassination by mafia networks serving French interests in Africa (Françafrique).

Whatever the arguments for or against maintaining the CFA franc, one thing is certain, it has contributed neither to the development of African member countries, nor to their economic integration. There are three main reasons for this: 1) The franc zone traps France's former colonies in a monetary arrangement over which they exercise no sovereignty. Thus, they exercise no right to use it as an instrument of economic policy in the event of external or internal shocks; 2) The operating principles of the franc zone mortgage the development potential of these countries by allowing for massive capital flight and control by French and western companies over African member economies; 3) The CFA franc does not reflect the fundamentals of the economies of these countries. This is illustrated by the price structure that has little to do with the standard of living member states. But, before analysing these policies, let us look first at the nature of money and how currency is used by France to protect its own interests and perpetuate its domination in the region.

The nature of money

Money is at the heart of the modern economy. The evocation of the 'money war' between China and western countries, including the US, is an eloquent illustration of the key role played by money in the economy of a country and in international economic and financial relations.

Functions of money

Economic theory assigns three functions to money: as a unit of account, as a medium of exchange and as a store of value. The unit of account function (or cash, standard of values) compares the economic variables, giving each a monetary value. The intermediary trade function allows transactions between goods and services. This feature eliminates barter, which is the direct exchange of physical quantities of goods and is a difficult and complicated process, the limitations of which are evident. Finally, a store of value gives the currency a dynamic nature, a temporality and, indeed, makes it a link between the present and the future.

These functions provide a utilitarian nature to money. But money is more than that. It has a social and political dimension, because it influences the daily acts of individuals. So, beyond its functional dimensions, money plays a role as social connector, hence, the primacy of money in social relations. Karl Marx (1972) showed that behind the production and circulation of goods, social relations are expressed. But money is a commodity unike any other. It is the general equivalent, the standard by which all other goods are measured. Therefore, it is the most complete expression of social relations. So, money has an important social dimension which cannot be explained by its functional attributes. Some economists argue that money is an instrument of socialisation for individuals. Money is classified as an institution, the primary mission of which is to serve the public good. Conceived as such, money is a public good that is essential for any society and cannot be privatised. These attributes explain why the issue of money is the sole responsibility of the state as symbol of its collective will.

Money: symbol of a country's sovereignty

Money is a symbol of sovereignty, a symbol that is reinforced by its social and political dimension. The power to coin money has always been recognised as an attribute of national sovereignty. Over time, the privilege of issuing currencies emerged as an attribute of sovereignty exemplified by the phrase 'money is the sole preserve of the Prince'. Indeed, the creation of a national currency is among the first assertions of sovereignty after a country wins freedom and transitions to independence. That is why only the state – as a symbol of public authority – has the exclusive right to issue the currency used throughout the territory under its jurisdiction (Ruffini 1996).

So, the currency, just like the flag or the national anthem, is one of the symbols that express the sovereignty of a country. And that sovereignty cannot be granted: it is won through struggle. In the current global crisis, the countries that exercise full monetary sovereignty have more room to manoeuvre; by using adjustments in monetary policies (exchange rate, interest rate) they better cope with the crisis.

Since the outbreak of the global financial crisis in September 2008, the US and European countries, as well as China, have injected massive amounts of money into their respective economies, in attempts to limit the impact of the crisis and boost their economies. The US Federal Reserve, for example, took the unprecedented step to fluctuate the discount rate between 0 and 0.25 per cent until end of 2013, in order to support its anaemic economy. The European Central Bank (ECB) is not far behind. Despite the aversion of Germany to the intervention of the ECB, it has decided to buy the debts of troubled European countries in order to prevent the collapse of their economies and the risk of collapse of the euro zone.

Franc zone: instrument of control

The best evidence that African countries have no sovereignty over the CFA franc is demonstrated in the nature of the relations between these countries and France from 1960 to the present day.

Repression against disobedient African leaders

A classic illustration of the nature of the franc zone as an instrument of domination and violation resides in the fate of the countries that left, or tried to leave, the zone following independence. With few exceptions, the leaders who attempted this were subject to fierce repression, ranging from sabotage and systematic demonisation (Guinea) to murder (Togo) and coup d'état (Mali).

After voting 'No' in the referendum of 1958, which opened the door to independence, Guinea decided to issue its own currency. Feeling humiliated, France triggered a merciless political, economic and psychological war against Sékou Touré's regime, with the complicity of countries, such as Côte d'Ivoire and Senegal. This was in an effort to derail the Guinean experience and deter other countries from following its example.

But that did not stop Sylvanus Olympio, the first president of Togo, from trying to follow suit. For his trouble, he was assassinated in a coup d'état instigated by France in 1963, which brought to power Gnassimbé Eyadema, a former soldier in the colonial army. Eyadema remained in power for nearly 40 years, becoming one of the pillars of the Françafrique, along with Houphouët-Boigny in Côte d'Ivoire and Senghor in Senegal. Modibo Keita of Mali was a victim of a coup in 1968 that sent him to prison until his death. A few years later, Keita's replacement, General Moussa Traoré, a former officer of the French colonial army, reintegrated Mali into the franc zone.

The humiliation of franc zone African leaders

The devaluation of the CFA franc in January 1994 was probably the most humiliating episode and the most striking evidence that African countries do not exercise monetary sovereignty. The heads of state and government entourages of these countries were sequestered for hours at a hotel in Dakar by the France's minister of cooperation, the director of the treasury[57] and the director general of the International Monetary Fund (IMF), who informed them of the decision by France and the IMF to devalue the currency. The vicissitudes were described by a newspaper as follows: 'In Dakar, 14 African Heads of State and Government gathered for thirty hours in hostage situation, forced to sign in order to regain their freedom.' (Dembele 2008)

Did they learn anything from this terrible humiliation? Unfortunately not, because to date, the franc zone system prevails. African countries are continuously deprived of their monetary sovereignty. The proclaimed 'independence' of the Central Bank of West African States (BCEAO) and the reform of 2010, did little to enhance real monetary sovereignty. Indeed, a Monetary Policy Committee (MPC), responsible for the definition and conduct of the monetary policies and set up as part of the reform process is governed by a committee – members of which include a representative of France's treasury with voting rights and the president of the West African Economic and Monetary Union (WAEMU – representing eight African countries[58]) who enjoys an advisory role. This largely explains why the monetary policies of the BCEAO and its counterpart in Central Africa – the Bank of Central African States (BEAC) – are not focused on the development needs and priorities of member countries, but rather modelled on those of the monetarist policies of the ECB.

---

57. Note that neither then president François Mitterrand, nor his prime minister, Edouard Balladur, deigned to make the trip to Dakar.
58. Benin, Burkina Faso, Côte d'Ivoire, Guinea-Bissau, Mali, Niger, Senegal and Togo.

Monetary policies of African central banks

There are two schools of thought that dominate economic policy in the post-war period in the West and its dependents. These include the Keynesian school, named after John Maynard Keynes, the great British economist whose ideas strongly influenced development policies in the West until the early 1970s. From the mid-1970s the monetarist school strongly influenced economic policy in the West and in many countries of the South, especially those that are tied to contracts with the World Bank and the IMF. The influence of the monetarist creed, as well as institutional links with France, are far reaching and impact negatively on the development interests of franc zone member countries. The BCEAO and BEAC continue to impose restrictive monetary policies that are intended to fight inflation but consequently limit the financing of government budget deficits and at the expense of increased productive capacity.

For example, the objectives of the institutional reforms introduced in April 2010, were aptly described by Philippe-Henri Dacoury-Tabley, the former governor of the BCEAO: 'The implementation of the reform – by assigning the BCEAO a primary objective of price stability – should contribute to guarantee the purchasing power of our currency and provide an adequate response to the challenge of financing economies.'[59] Note the emphasis on 'price stability'. It is difficult to understand why the central bank of among the poorest developing countries prioritises the fight against inflation at the expense of economic development through job creation and poverty eradication. This is even more absurd than the concern of the BCEAO that? the fight against inflation is groundless. Indeed, it is based on the monetarist dogma that relates inflation to excess money supply. But critics of this approach argue that inflation in the WAEMU zone is not of monetary origin; that the main source of inflation in the region is imported from the euro zone – the WAEMU's largest trading partner. The second source is cost inflation, mainly due to imports of

59. Interviewed on March 31, 2010. See also Le Monde Diplomatique, July 2010, p. 12

crude oil. For example, increases in oil prices almost automatically result in higher cost of production in the net oil-importing countries. The third source of inflation in WAEMU countries is inflation resulting from exogenous shocks (drought, floods), which result in poor harvests that result in soaring food prices, and therefore inflation induced by food shortages (Dembele 2010).

A study by James Heintz and Léonce Ndikumana (2010) questions the policies targeting inflation as the primary objective to the detriment of other goals, such as growth, job creation and poverty eradication. Indeed, such a policy could tie the hands of the central bank and remove every possibility of undertaking anti-cyclical policies when exogenous or endogenous shocks occur, such as the structural problems of low domestic supply capacity, particularly in the food industry. In fact, the study gives several examples showing that double-digit inflation, up to 12 percent, is quite compatible with sustained growth.

Reducing financing for government deficits

In 2002, the BCEAO deleted Article 16 of its statute, which allowed for the financing members states up to 20 per cent of the previous year tax revenues. This condemned the LCD states to depend on external public or private financing sources (issuance of treasury bills and bonds in the financial markets) or stringent loans from international financial institutions that are known to exacerbate poverty in these countries. As such, the monetary policies of the central banks of African member states became an obstacle to economic and social transformation, while exacerbating external dependence and creating further barriers to sovereignty.

Franc zone and the underdevelopment of African countries

To recap, the franc zone is based on the following four pillars:

> 1) Fixed parity exchange rates between the CFA franc of the two African sub-regions (Central Africa and West Africa).
>
> 2) The guarantee of unlimited convertibility by the French treasury for currencies issued by different institutions of the franc zone.
>
> 3) Freedom of transfer within the area. Within each sub-region and between each of them and France, there is freedom of capital transfers; so, no exchange controls.
>
> 4) The centralisation of foreign exchange reserves, which is done at two levels. States centralise their foreign exchange reserves at each of the two central banks. In return for the unlimited convertibility guaranteed by France, the BCEAO and BEAC are required to deposit 50 per cent of their net foreign exchange reserves in transaction accounts within the French treasury. Imagine, half of the foreign exchange reserves of the ECB placed at the Federal Reserve of the United States? What autonomy would the ECB then have to conduct its monetary policy?

Supporters of the franc zone monetary system argue that African member states benefit in several ways, including: through the development of macroeconomic stability; the absence of exchange rate risk, which creates a favourable environment for foreign direct investment; and the promotion of integration of member countries. But experience shows that the operating principles of the franc zone and the peg to the euro by a fixed exchange rate are obstacles to development countries. For example, the principle of a fixed exchange rate with a hard currency like the euro is a major handicap for African economies. Due to the fixed exchange rate, the African central banks have little leeway in case of exogenous shocks, such as changes in the commodity prices exported by African countries or increased production costs resulting in loss of competitiveness on foreign markets.

The principle of centralising half of reserves in France deprives African countries of valuable resources to finance their development. Moreover, the operating principles of the area are such that the banking system of member countries participates very little in financing African businesses. One of the reasons for this is that the banking system is poorly developed, especially within the WAEMU. Moreover, citizens take little interest to the banking system, which explains the very low rate of use of banking services in the countries of the zone. For example, according to the BCEAO, in 2005 only three per cent of the citizens of this area had access to a bank account. This low rate prompted the BCEAO to undertake a comprehensive awareness campaign in all member countries to encourage people to open accounts. In order to support this campaign, some countries like Senegal, decided that all those who are paid by the state, including students entitled to scholarships, are required to open bank accounts.

As for the financing of economies by banks, it represents only 16 per cent of the gross domestic product (GDP) in Cote d'Ivoire, a country whose economy accounts for about 40 per cent of the WAEMU. In comparison, in Tunisia the rate is about 70 per cent. The majority of banks in the WAEMU zone have large amounts of cash at their disposal, but it is used for short-term financing, such as consumer credit or home loans, at the expense of long-term investments in key sectors of the economy and infrastructure to help improve the productive apparatus.

This excess liquidity is paradoxical and even absurd, given the enormous financing needs of African economies. Moreover, it has an impact on the conduct of the monetary policy by the central bank. According to experts, in the presence of abundant excess liquidity, monetary policy faces several challenges which penalise efficiency. The presence of a non- or low-paid liquidity weighs on the profitability of the banking system, making it more vulnerable and contributing to increased costs of borrowing. Excess liquidity makes the monetary policy passive and leaves little room for manoeuvre. (Dufrénot 2012). This impotence of the monetary policy can also be observed in the movement of capital.

The franc zone and capital flows

Indeed, the four principles that impact the economics of the franc zone, including the free movement of capital between African countries and France, remove any control on capital movements within the area by the central banks. Thus, we are witnessing massive capital flight out of the franc zone, especially during times of political or economic crises. This has led to massive repatriation of profits by foreign investors to their parent-companies and a flight of the income of expatriate households to their country of origin. Thus, between 1970 and 1993, while foreign investment in African countries of the franc zone was estimated at $1.7 billion, the repatriation of profits and expatriate income was estimated at $6.3 billion during the same period, nearly four times the level of foreign investment (Agbohou 1999).

These figures largely invalidate the view that the stability of the franc zone promotes FDI. African countries that receive the most direct investment are those that are rich in oil and mineral resources, not necessarily those with 'stable' currencies. Even countries like Tanzania and Mozambique receive more FDI than the member countries of the franc zone (Dembele op.cit.). This is confirmed by the figures in Table 1.

Table 1: FDI flows compared between CFA & non-CFA countries ($ per capita)

Countries or regions	2001	2005	2006	2007	2008
Angola	145.9	408.9	530.4	558.0	862.0
Cameroon	4.5	12.6	16.9	15.2	13.6
Congo	23.0	150.3	550.6	511.4	725.0
Côte d'Ivoire	15.4	16.2	16.2	21.2	17.1
Gabon	-70.6	177.0	191.9	189.4	14.0
Ghana	4.5	6.6	26.4	37.4	90.8
Mali	11.3	18.9	6.9	5.9	10.0
Mozambique	13.6	5.2	7.2	19.5	26.2
Niger	2.0	2.3	3.7	9.1	10.0
Nigeria	10.0	35.0	96.7	84.3	134.1
Senegal	3.1	4.0	19.0	25.0	57.8

Source: ADB, Statistical yearbook 2010, table 3-6, p. 65

Franc zone and sub-regional integration

Contrary to the claims of its proponents, the CFA franc has not contributed to the integration of member countries. In 2008, as shown in Table 2, trade within WAEMU did not exceed 15 per cent on average for exports and was less than 10 per cent for imports. In addition, these exchanges are concentrated in three countries: Côte d'Ivoire, Mali and Senegal.

Still in 2008, the WAEMU countries sold a little more than twice to other member countries of the Economic Community of the West African (ECOWAS) (28.3%) than they bought from them (12.9%). The Economic and Monetary Community of Central Africa (CEMAC), intra-community trade was insignificant at 0.8 per cent and 2.5 per cent respectively for exports and imports. Overall, the table shows that trade between member countries of the franc zone is low, with exports of 5.2 per cent and imports up to 6.5 per cent of their total trade.

Table 2: Trade data for 2008 (% of total trade)

Exports to (%)	CEMAC	ECOWAS	WAEMU	FRANC ZONE	AFRICA
CEMAC	0.8	0.9	0.5	17.1	2.4
ECOWAS	1.4	8.0	4.6	5.9	11.7
WAEMU	2.1	28.3	14.9	17.1	14.4
FRC ZONE	1.2	7.9	4.1	5.2	10.5
Imports from (%)	CEMAC	ECOWAS	WAEMU	FRANC ZONE	AFRICA
CEMAC	2.5	2.6	1.1	3.7	7.5
ECOWAS	1.3	7.4	4.3	5.6	11.2
WAEMU	1.0	12.9	6.8	7.8	15.9
FRC ZONE	1.5	9.8	5.1	6.5	13.3

Source: Statistical Yearbook 2010 of the ADB, Table 3-7, p. 66

The poor intra-African trade is partly explained by the structure of their exports, which consist mainly of commodities. Furthermore, the liberalisation policies imposed by the World Bank and IMF for more than three decades have contributed to the destruction of the few processing industries established in the 1960s and 1970s. The result was widespread poverty in member countries of the franc zone, as shown in the rankings in Table 3. In fact, out of 15 member countries of the franc zone (including the Comoros), 11 are ranked among Least Developed Countries (UNCTAD 2010) and three as Heavily Indebted Poor Countries (HIPC) by the World Bank and the IMF. Gabon is the only country that escapes either category.

Table 3: Status of Franc Zone Member Countries

Countries	UN Ranking	IMF ranking
Benin	LDC	HIPC
Burkina Faso	LDC	HIPC
Cameroon	-	HIPC
Comoros	LDC	HIPC
Congo	-	HIPC
Côte d'Ivoire	-	HIPC
Gabon	-	-
Guinea-Bissau	LDC	HIPC
Equatorial Guinea	LDC	HIPC
Mali	LDC	HIPC
Niger	LDC	HIPC
CAR	LDC	HIPC
Senegal	LDC	HIPC
Chad	LDC	HIPC
Togo	LDC	HIPC

Source: IMF Classification

What future for the CFA franc?

It is clear that the CFA franc is an instrument of control that hampers any prospect of emancipation and development of African countries. The creation of sovereign currencies is one of the essential components of developmental states in Africa, the urgency and necessity of which have been highlighted in recent years in order to promote effective policies of inward-looking economic and social transformation (CEA 2011, UNCTAD 2007). Therefore, sustainable development in these countries is dependent on the demise of the CFA franc and its replacement by sub-regional, sovereign currencies. In other words, the developmental state is incompatible with the absence of monetary sovereignty. It is time that African countries of the franc zone learn the lessons from history and learn from ongoing examples to create their own currency and make it a real tool for economic and social transformation.

Conclusion

After more than 50 years of failed independence, African leaders are facing a dilemma: continue to be trapped in the franc zone or pursue economic emancipation by exiting the zone and its monetary restrictions, with the supportive measures and policies needed to carry out such a venture. Admittedly, this will not be an easy task, and sacrifices will be required. The world is undergoing profound changes, marked by the systemic crisis of capitalism that some liken to a crisis of civilisation, the emergence of new paradigms and the gestation of a new international monetary and financial architecture, with the rise of China and other BRICS and the relative decline of Western powers (CEA 2011, Dufrénot op.cit.). In this context, African countries of the franc zone cannot afford to maintain the status quo. They must finally turn the page of the CFA franc and opt for the creation of a sovereign currency to achieve their economic and social development. The decisions to establish an African Monetary Fund, an African Central Bank and an African Investment Bank represent significant steps in the process of integration, which is essential for laying the foundation for development.

In the words of Jean Ping, the former president of the AU Commission: 'we now know that the capitalist market will not solve everything and that nothing is irreversible. Nobody can dictate anymore what we have to do... Africa must first rely on itself...' (Jeune Afrique 2009: 18)

References

Agbohou, N. (2008) *Le Franc CFA et l'Euro contre l'Afrique*, Paris, Editions Solidarité Mondiale

Dembélé, D.M (2010) 'Le franc Cfa en sursis' in Le Monde Diplomatique, July

– (2008) 'Monnaie, souveraineté et développement économique en Afrique : préparer la levée de l'hypothèque du franc Cfa', Perspective Africaine, No. 2, pp. 172–83

Dufrénot, G. (2012) 'The CFA franc in the face of the Eurozone troubles', African Geopolitics, No. 43, Second quarter, pp.187–97

ECA (2011) Reform of the international financial architecture and its impact on Africa, ECA Policy Research, No. 1, Addis Ababa

Fanon, Frantz (2002) [1961], *Les damnés de la terre*, Paris, La Découverte/Poche

Heinz, J. and Ndikumana, L. (2010) 'Is there a case for formal inflation targeting in sub-Saharan Africa?' AfDB Group Working Paper Series No. 108, April

Jeune Afrique, 15-21 November 2009, p.18

Marx, K. (1972) [1859] *Contribution à la critique de l'économie politique*, Paris, Editions Sociales

Ruffini, Pierre-Bruno (1996) Les théories monétaires, Paris, Editions du Seuil

Tchundjang Pouémi, J. (2000) [1981] *Monnaie, servitude et liberté: la répression monétaire de l'Afrique'*, Paris, Editions Ménaibuc

UNCTAD (2010) The Least Developed Countries Report 2010, United Nations, New York and Geneva

MONETARY INTEGRATION IN WEST AFRICA: THE WAY TO THE ECOWAS SINGLE CURRENCY
Mohamed Ben Omar Ndiaye

Introduction

Economic integration is the process by which many nations agree to facilitate trade between each other in order to gradually unify their markets, and draw mutual benefits. According to François Perroux (1969), 'the act of integrating brings elements together to form a whole, or reinforces the coherence of a whole lot already existing'. Regional economic and monetary integration in Africa is now seen as an effective way not only to eradicate poverty and promote development, but also to cushion the potential systemic effects of the process of economic globalisation.

In West Africa, the Economic Community of West African States (ECOWAS) is still struggling to achieve economic integration, despite the adoption of the ECOWAS Monetary Cooperation Programme (EMCP) more than 20 years ago. Although some good performances have been recorded for some macroeconomic indicators, including some economic convergence criteria, disparities persist both between the different economies of the member states within each zone, and between the West African Monetary Union (UEMOA) and the West African Monetary Zone (WAMZ). This justifies the many concerns about the ECOWAS monetary union project.

The theory of optimum currency areas: baseline

Definition of the currency area

There is no universally accepted definition of the concept of monetary integration. In general, a monetary area involves at least two countries within which exchange rates are fixed, currencies are convertible between each other or even the same currency, foreign reserves are pooled, a central bank and/or other public economic policy agencies exist and floating exchange rates are adopted.

The criterion of mobility of factors – an overview

According to Robert Mundell (1961), a currency area is optimal when mobility of factors within the zone is greater than what appears vis-à-vis the external world.

Ronald McKinnon (1963) argued that a high degree of openness is the criterion for the development of an optimal currency area. He said that if the economy is not too open, the change in the exchange rate can significantly improve the balance of payments.

Peter Kenen (1969) believed that an economy that has a diversified productive structure (both from geographical and sectoral perspectives) has the means to offset the adverse effects (inflation, unemployment) caused by the instability of certain products. In terms of the level of financial integration, work around this criterion refers on the one hand to public financial integration (or fiscal integration) and on the other hand to private financial integration.

Harry Johnson (1970) concluded that two regions (countries) that are highly integrated for tax purposes will be able to form an OCA, to the extent that the federal budget can play the stabilising role for real income, on the one hand, and exchange rates on the other hand.

James Ingram and Tibor Scitovsky (1969) argued that the stronger the financial integration, the more interest rate differentials, and hence exchange rates, are reduced. Thus, the countries in question have more interest in participating in a monetary union and staying in a fixed exchange rate regime because financial flows will compensate for deficits in the balance of payments.

The shift from Mundell: from the convergence of inflation rates to the 'neoHayekian' theory of competing currencies.

Gottfried Harberler (1970), J. Marcus Fleming (1971) and Paul de Grauwe (1975) believed that would an optimal currency area is an area in which there is a similarity of inflation rates

Ingram (1969), Harberler (1970), Edward Tower and Thomas D. Willet (1970) stated that it is not economic criteria that matter in defining an optimal currency area, but rather the consistency of economic policies among member countries and their ability to address inflation and growth.

Henri Bourguinat (1973) thinks that any proposed monetary union should be subject to two conditions: acceptable circulation of an asset within the area and the community, or, at least, close national preferences in terms of significant changes in inflation rates, real wages, productivity, etc.

Charles Kindleberger (1986) added that the necessary conditions of a monetary union included an institutionalised agreement between member countries on one or more major preferences on the key objectives of convergence and internal stability.

The 'NeoHayekian' theory on competing currencies

This theory is based on the idea that competition between currencies (banking and public sector), or even between foreign currencies, ensures that states avoid maintaining inflation to promote trust and economic growth. The differentiation of currencies is not an obstacle to the free movement of goods, currencies or financial assets. So it is not necessary to have a single currency, but, rather one or more 'good currencies' with stable and/or undifferentiated purchasing power.

Recent developments for optimal monetary unions

Cost-benefit analysis

This approach recognises three benefits to the monetary union: improvement of the cash value of the currency, the elimination of foreign exchange speculation, and the elimination of the management costs of external resources. Nevertheless, the costs attached to the monetary union include giving up exchange rate manipulation, the risk of polarised growth, the loss of independent monetary policy, or even the fiscal policy. Projected in the long-term, the dynamic gains of a union outweigh the costs that, by nature, are transient (Fratianni, Von Hagen 1992).

Why choose the single currency from the process of adjustment to supply and demand related shocks? The methodology used here is to review the following correlated questions:

♦ Are the countries that intend to form a monetary union experiencing the convergence of inflation and growth rates?

♦ What is the response time of these countries when faced with shocks to supply and demand?

♦ Faced with strong constraints on monetary policies, are the responses by the union member countries similar?

The level of flexibility of factors in an uncertain environment

William Branson (1989) shows that in a world of uncertainty, the irrevocable fixing of exchange rates (exchange rate stability) makes fiscal policies more efficient, increases mobility of factors (workers) and helps stabilise the production variance.

Philips' curve: independence of the central bank and the credibility of monetary policy in favour of the OCA

The achievement of an optimum currency area has evolved to comparing the Philips curves of member states, the independence of the central bank, or to the idea of optimal contracts between central banks and government authorities, thus demonstrating an interest for the conservative central banker who targets low inflation. This objective must be met for each country even before the transition to the monetary union. So, one way to foster credibility (irreversible trust) is to 'tie one's hands' by delegating the monetary policy to a central bank, which imposes a discipline on all member countries of a union (e.g. Guinea Bissau joining the BCEAO in May 1997).

De Grauwe (1992) considers that 'the most significant abrupt shift for a country is to join a monetary union with a country with a negligible inflation'.

The level of coordination of fiscal and monetary policies

In one application for developing countries, Pierre-Richard Agenor (1991) concluded that 'joining a monetary union is a way to pursue a monetary policy that enhances the reputation of authorities'.

The degree of solidarity between candidates for OCA

Albert Ondo Ossa (2000) considers that any member of a 'solidarity' zone is liable for the actions of other members – in other words, for their surpluses and deficits. In order for there to be a single currency between two countries, it is necessary for the deficit in one county to be offset by a surplus in the other. And therefore, both countries must agree on the policies and a method of managing their foreign assets in such a way to restore equilibrium in their balance of payments.

The exchange rate stability

Proponents of this approach believe that countries that can form a monetary union are those with stable bilateral exchange rates over a long period. This belief is based on the central assumption that exchange rates are stable when countries are facing similar shocks.

Political will

Jerome Mintz (1970) considers that political will is the only, if not the most important, requirement for the formation of an optimal currency union. Manfred Willms (1994) concurs that only political commitment can ensure the sustainability of a currency area.

The theoretical foundations of economic convergence

For two decades, the new formulations in the theory of optimum currency unions have promoted harmonisation procedures leading to the convergence criteria of economies. The review of the process of economic convergence is the subject of the work by many economists.

The traditional growth theory predicts that similar economies in terms of technology and preferences would converge towards the same level of GDP per capita. In contrast, the theory of endogenous growth initiated by Paul Romer (1986) states that the differences between the levels of GDP per capita will persist. Faced with this theoretical debate, several attempts have emerged to test the implications of the two types of model. Three competing hypotheses were developed:

♦ **The assumption of absolute convergence:** national income per capita converge to a long-term identical level regardless of the initial conditions.

♦ **The hypothesis of conditional convergence:** per capita income of regions with identical characteristics (for instance in terms of preferences, technology, population growth rate, or public policies) converge to the same long-term level regardless of their initial position.

♦ **The assumption of club convergence** (supporting the concepts of polarisation, poverty trap): per capita income of regions with identical structural characteristics converges to an identical long-term level provided that the initial conditions of these regions are close enough.

Empirical tests of the hypotheses of economic convergence generally lead to three important outcomes:

♦ Rejection of the hypothesis of absolute convergence
♦ Robustness of the conditional convergence hypothesis
♦ Detection of club convergence and the existence of multiple equilibriums.

The analysis of these assumptions of convergence and the empirical tests results highlight the following lessons:

♦ It will be difficult, if not impossible to achieve (absolute) global convergence in the long term for countries with different structural characteristics, for example, in terms of technology, preferences, population growth, public policy, market structures, etc.
♦ Convergence can only exist when a number of prerequisites have been previously achieved (conditional convergence).

All these lessons confirm the great difficulty in implementing the convergence criteria. To create an EMU, shall we start coordinating economic policies and gradually integrate the economies (argument defended by economists)? Or, on the contrary, immediately start the monetary union (argument defended by monetarists)? Here, it is not a matter of the chicken-and-egg type academic debate, whether the monetary union should come before economic integration or vice versa. In the first case, the move towards the EMU will be gradual and long. In the second case, the monetary union will be created quickly with the idea that it will impose such a constraint on member countries that they must necessarily coordinate and integrate their economies.

Review of compliance of the ECOWAS zone in regard of the OCA and economic convergence criteria

The purpose of this section is to try to assess the efficiencies of economic integration in terms of optimality and convergence of the economies in the ECOWAS region. More specifically, it will address three main questions:

- ◆ What is the level of conformity of the ECOWAS region with the baseline conditions for an optimal currency union?
- ◆ Is there macroeconomic stability in terms of economic convergence?
- ◆ Is compliance with the criteria of optimum currency area and economic convergence a prerequisite without which no common currency creation is possible?

ECOWAS under the requirements of an OMU

◆ *Mobility of production factors*

Significant efforts have been made by adopting many legal instruments to remove obstacles to the free movement of persons, goods, services and capital, for the right of residence and establishment in view of establishing a customs and economic union in the ECOWAS region. However, these efforts are limited by the lack of infrastructure to support the implementation of the protocols promoting freedom of movement.

♦ *Similarity of shocks*

According to a study conducted by Paul Mason and Catherine Pattillo (2001), ECOWAS countries experience asymmetric shocks.

♦ *Openness of economies*

The level of openness of the economies in the ECOWAS is about 55 per cent. Intra-regional trade is about 10 per cent. However, official statistics do not take into account informal trade that is increasingly gaining momentum. Overall, the economic structure of the region is not conducive to rapid development of regional trade, and most ECOWAS countries are commodity exporters, and importers of manufactured goods.

♦ *Financial integration*

The financial zone of the ECOWAS is not integrated either in the public or private sector. Financial markets do not yet exist at the ECOWAS level, nor has a legal framework been finalised. Fiscal policies are not currently harmonised. The reality is that no member country has a sufficiently large economic space to develop monetary and financial markets at the national level. This is the whole point about creating a regional ECOWAS market.

♦ *Nature of specialisation*

The structure of production is on average poorly diversified within ECOWAS. Countries such as Guinea, Nigeria, Niger, and Guinea-Bissau derive more than 50 per cent of their export earnings from a single commodity.

◆ *Similarity of inflation rates*

Apart from WAEMU countries that share a common currency, prices are rising inconsistently in the ECOWAS region.

◆ *Instability of exchange rates*

Based on monthly changes in ECOWAS currency exchange rates with respect to the WAUA over the 2004–2007 period, it appears that the variability of exchange rates is very low. It is noted that with the exception of the Guinean franc and to a lesser extent, the Liberian dollar, the variability of ECOWAS currencies is on a small scale in the period under review.

◆ *Political commitment*

If we consider the commitment of ECOWAS authorities to adopt legal and regulatory instruments, there is political will at all levels for achieving the ECOWAS Monetary Union. However, we must recognise that some are struggling to meet their contractual commitments on the harmonisation of policies and macroeconomic convergence due to internal problems. Compliance with the criteria can be used to assess progress towards achieving macroeconomic convergence.

The ECOWAS region in light of macroeconomic convergence requirements

Overall budget deficit to GDP

At the end of 2010, the performance of ECOWAS member states with respect to this criterion was mixed. Countries such as Benin, Côte d'Ivoire, Liberia and Nigeria often met this criterion. On the other hand, Burkina Faso, Cape Verde, Ghana, Guinea Bissau, Niger and Sierra Leone failed to meet this criterion over the period 2000–2010 and other countries in the region performed erratically.

Inflation

Over the period 2000-2010, three ECOWAS countries namely Burkina Faso, Côte d'Ivoire and Niger always managed to keep inflation within the five per cent limit. On the other hand, Benin, Cape Verde, Mali and Senegal only failed to meet this criterion in a single year. However, Ghana, Guinea and Nigeria have never been able to meet this criterion, although efforts were registered for these countries over the same period.

Budget deficit financing by the central bank

Since 2005 failures to meet this criterion were rare.

Gross foreign exchange reserves

Since the introduction of the convergence program, compliance with this criterion has been problematic. Indeed, apart from the WAEMU countries that meet this criterion as a block, and Nigeria, other countries are experiencing difficulties in relation to the six-months imports coverage requirement.

ECOWAS and practical cases of monetary unions

In respect of monetary unions, the euro area and the CFA in Africa are indeed striking examples:

♦ *Case of the Economic and Monetary Union (EMU)*

Today, the euro zone is a benchmark for monetary integration. Yet, most studies in this area disclosed that the euro zone is not optimal. Thus, for authors such as Willms (1994) and many others, the creation of the European Economic and Monetary Union (EMU) was not based solely on economic criteria. In this case, only political factors can explain the creation of the EMU. The Maastricht Treaty assumes that the stability of exchange rates and prices will promote growth, and trade between member states, and that these exchanges, in turn, will promote the approximation of their structures and their levels of development; growth being more favoured by the stability of economic policies than by their more or less expansionary nature.

♦ *Case of the West Africa Economic and Monetary Union (WAEMU)*

Experience shows that the convergence process should be continued after the adoption of a common currency – the CFA franc. In this context, the conduct of a common monetary policy seems to favour the achievement of convergence (e.g. control of inflation rates).

Key lessons from the ECOWAS optimality and macroeconomic convergence

At present, the ideal conditions (baseline) for a monetary union are not met by ECOWAS. Performance in terms of convergence of economies is low. Experiences of economic and monetary integration have shown that, in practice, no monetary union meets the criteria for optimal currency area. The explanation is that the criteria to recognise an optimum currency and convergence area are a set of ideal conditions, a baseline (or limit) which candidate economies for a union should aim at. Moreover, macroeconomic convergence is an ongoing process that must be constantly sought and pursued after the creation of the single currency, which in turn facilitates this convergence.

ECOWAS Monetary Cooperation Programme (EMCP): issues, challenges and outlook on the single currency

Creation of ECOWAS: May 1975

♦ *Objectives*

Promote cooperation and integration for the creation of an economic union in West Africa to raise the standard of living of its peoples, maintain and enhance economic stability, foster relations between member states and contribute to the progress and development of the African continent.

In pursuing these objectives, the harmonisation of policies in the monetary, financial and payments policies has always been considered an important step (Article 51 b of the ECOWAS Treaty). However, the existence of eight non-convertible currencies in the region is a major handicap, hence, the need for monetary cooperation to facilitate the creation of an economic union.

Genesis of ECOWAS monetary cooperation

West African Clearing House (WACH)	ECOWAS Multilateral Clearing Mechanism (EMCM)
The WACH was created in March 1976 (it began operations in July 1976) to manage the ECOWAS multilateral clearing mechanism (EMCM) with the objective to promote inter-ECOWAS trade	The EMCM was a multilateral monetary arrangement for payments and transfers related to current account transactions (visible and invisible trade) within the community.

Overall, the wach was to the the following:

- ♦ Serving as a channel through which member countries could use their national currencies for intra-regional trade and make savings in the use of foreign reserves.
- ♦ Simplifying the settlement of commercial transactions through a system of multilateral clearing and settlement of net positions at the end of each month.

The system worked well initially with a value of transactions which had a tendency to increase, reaching 291.2 million dollars in 1985, but later on, the value had dropped drastically to 6.8 million in 2002 before it closed in 2004.

- ♦ The failure of the clearing mechanism has been attributed to a number of factors including:

- ♦ Operational difficulties (instability of the exchange rate, poor telecommunications, delay in transaction processing, etc.)

- ♦ Accumulation of substantial arrears payable in foreign currency

- ♦ Improvement of payment systems in some countries.

ECOWAS Monetary Cooperation Programme (EMCP)

Adoption in July 1987 of a framework for monetary and financial cooperation among member countries; the ultimate goal being the creation of a single currency within the ECOWAS.

Member countries must adopt common policy measures for the implementation of a stable macroeconomic and harmonised monetary environment:

- ♦ compliance with the prescribed macroeconomic convergence criteria
- ♦ harmonisation of fiscal, monetary and financial policies

♦ adoption of a market-based exchange rate regime

♦ liberalisation of the monetary, capital and labour markets

♦ creation of an effective community market through trade liberalisation within the community.

ECOWAS Monetary Cooperation Programme

1996	♦ Transformation of the WACH into the WAMA to manage the EMCP ♦ In addition to the functions of the WACH, WAMA was mandated: 1. to promote monetary cooperation and consultation between member states 2. to assist member states in the harmonisation and coordination of monetary and fiscal policies and their structural adjustment programs 3. monitor, coordinate and implement the EMCP 4. to undertake studies on how to better support the economic and monetary integration of ECOWAS.

1999/0	♦ Approval of a number of policy measures to accelerate the integration process, including: 1. extension of macroeconomic criteria from four to 10, grouped into primary criteria (4) and secondary (6) criteria 2. adoption of the Fast Track Initiative, which includes a plan to create a second monetary zone (WAMZ) 3. declaration of intent, in 2000, by the heads of state of six West African countries outside the CFA zone and Cape Verde, to create the WAMZ and launch a common currency in this area in 2003.
2001	♦ The objective of the ECOWAS Multilateral Surveillance Mechanism with the primary and secondary convergence criteria (Decision/Dec 17/12/01) was to ensure closer coordination of economic policies and the convergence of national economies in order to create a viable economic and monetary union. ♦ The mechanism includes the following components: 1. The Convergence Board 2. The Technical Monitoring Committee 3. The Joint Secretariat 4. The National Coordinating Committees (NCCs)

Challenges to the EMCP and deferment

Progress under the EMCP was inadequate and could not support the launch of the monetary union.	The deadline for the materialisation of the programme was postponed several times: ♦ From 1998–2004 ♦ 2004–2020 The WAMZ project initiated under the EMCP has also been postponed several times: ♦ 2003–2005 ♦ 2005–2009 ♦ 2009–2015

New EMCP approach: approved roadmap for ECOWAS single currency

Background to the roadmap

Reflections on three proposed options: ♦ the big bang approach by a political decision ♦ pure, gradual approach based on a prior attainment of prescribed eligibility criteria ♦ The critical mass approach, that is to say that countries representing at least 75% of the ECOWAS GDP meet the primary convergence criteria	After review of the three options, the Convergence Board (at its meeting in October 2008) requested the ECOWAS Commission to conduct a study to determine the best option and the specific timetable for the introduction of the ECOWAS single currency.

Purpose of the roadmap

Setting the procedures for achieving the objective of the single currency.

Supporting the double-speed approach to the creation of the ECOWAS single currency:

- ♦ Step 1: Launch of the second monetary union (WAMZ) by 2015

- ♦ Step 2: merging the two sub-regional monetary unions – UEMOA and WAMZ – to achieve the ECOWAS single currency in 2020

Provide an overview of the range of planned activities and programmes to be implemented.

Summary of the roadmap content

	Key Activities	Timeframe
	Harmonisation of macroeconomic convergence criteria and operationalisation of NCCs/NEPCs as part of the multilateral surveillance mechanism	**2010**
	Harmonisation of regulation and supervision of banks and other financial institutions, the accounting and reporting framework of banks, of current account and capital transactions, the monetary policy framework and the infrastructure of payment systems	**2013**
	Alignment of statistics, domestic tax, legal, accounting and statistical framework of public finance	**2014**
	Introduction of the single currency in the WAMZ	**2015**
	Integration of financial markets and stabilisation of the exchange rate	**2018**
	Introduction of the ECOWAS single currency	**2020**

Architecture of the ECOWAS macroeconomic convergence criteria

The convergence criteria	**Primary criteria**	Fiscal deficit of no more than 4% of the GDP
		Inflation rate of no more than 5%
		Central bank deficit-financing of no more than 10% of the previous year's tax revenues
		Gross external reserves that can give import cover for a minimum of six months.
	Secondary criteria	Prohibition of new domestic default payments and liquidation of existing ones.
		Tax revenue should be equal to or greater than 20% of GDP.
		Wage bill to tax revenue equal to or less than 35%.
		Public investment to tax revenue equal to or greater than 20%
		A stable real exchange rate.
		A positive real interest rate

Performance under the macroeconomic convergence

	2000	2001	2002	2003	2004	2005	2006	2007	2008	2009	2010	2011	2012
Fiscal deficit	6	6	5	5	4	4	6	8	7	3	4	2	5
Inflation	11	9	10	10	9	9	9	7	1	10	7	7	0
External reserves	10	10	9	9	9	1	9	9	9	10	9	10	0
Central bank financing	12	13	11	11	14	15	13	15	13	12	12	11	0
Domestic default payments	4	4	3	4	4	3	8	4	5	8	9	9	0
Tax revenue	1	0	0	0	2	2	2	2	2	2	2	3	0
Wage bill	6	6	5	8	5	7	8	9	7	5	4	4	4
Investment to tax revenue	6	6	5	5	7	6	7	7	7	8	6	7	8
Real interest rate	12	6	8	9	7	7	6	6	0	11	4	4	0
Real exchange rate	-	11	12	7	12	10	12	2	4	11	5	10	10

	2000	2001	2002	2003	2004	2005	2006	2007	2008	2009	2010*
Benin	3	4	4	4	4	2	2	4	2	3	3
Burkina Faso	2	3	3	3	3	2	2	3	1	2	3
Cote d'Ivoire	3	4	4	4	4	3	3	4	2	3	4
Guinée-Bissau	1	3	3	3	3	2	2	2	1	2	3
Mali	2	2	3	3	3	2	2	3	1	3	3
Niger	2	3	3	3	3	2	2	3	1	2	3
Senegal	4	3	4	3	3	2	2	2	2	2	3
Togo	2	4	4	4	4	1	2	4	2	3	3
Gambie	3	1	0	0	1	2	3	2	0	2	2
Ghana	0	1	0	1	1	1	1	1	0	1	1
Guinee	0	2	0	0	0	2	1	2	2	0	1
Nigeria	3	2	2	2	3	3	3	3	3	3	3
Sierra Leone	1	1	2	0	1	1	0	1	1	0	0
Liberia	3	2	2	3	1	2	2	2	2	2	3
Cape Vert	1	2	2	2	2	2	2	3	1	2	2

Performance under the macroeconomic policy harmonisation

Exchange rate policy

Two exchange rate regimes still exist in West Africa:
- fixed exchange rates – UEMOA, Cape Verde
- floating exchange rates in other countries.

RER Misalignment of UEMOA Countries

Year	Benin	Burkina Faso	Cote D'Ivoire	Guinea Bissau	Mali	Niger	Senegal	Togo
1990	61.21	7.62	-1.74	-26.81	-2.71	13.10	-9.76	1.91
1991	70.01	10.66	-4.75	-20.45	0.22	16.86	-8.47	-1.80
1992	89.69	32.44	0.00	-6.06	-0.18	46.69	-15.14	-0.90
1993	97.38	36.91	1.07	-5.55	1.66	56.54	-11.56	-5.80
1994	-16.60	-35.08	-34.49	-47.25	-13.33	-29.38	-6.21	-34.37
1995	-9.36	-24.84	-21.52	-36.69	-10.92	-16.81	1.53	-24.57
1996	-8.05	-24.22	-19.17	-33.91	-9.09	-10.90	3.38	-23.34
1997	-17.62	-32.31	-19.83	-29.78	-9.29	-16.56	1.88	-22.14
1998	-17.95	-34.68	-14.38	-30.59	-8.39	-15.53	5.42	-15.83
1999	-18.01	-34.99	-15.62	-26.68	-8.13	-12.49	9.40	-16.37
2000	-28.65	-41.05	-20.90	-36.50	-7.96	-21.65	5.08	-15.46
2001	-30.78	-42.95	-18.84	-36.46	-7.13	-23.20	3.96	-10.00
2002	-27.30	-39.22	-16.79	-34.01	-7.71	-18.77	2.22	-5.89
2003	-13.35	-26.26	-13.14	-18.83	-11.63	1.60	2.48	-3.86
2004	-4.40	-16.00	-14.71	-11.72	11.44	12.76	-0.04	-5.15
2005	-8.13	-17.59	-17.07	-13.34	11.24	4.97	-5.34	-4.45
2006	-9.41	-14.53	-19.19	-10.29	6.42	5.28	-7.42	-6.19
2007	-7.34	-8.36	-18.37	-2.95	3.95	5.97	-6.29	-4.73
2008	-6.26	-3.73	-13.50	4.01	1.01	5.47	-5.57	4.60
2009	-4.06	0.93	-13.98	11.84	-1.07	6.29	-3.74	16.94
1990-1993	79.57	21.91	-1.35	-14.72	-0.25	33.30	-11.23	-1.65
1994-2009	-14.20	-24.68	-18.22	-22.07	-3.79	-7.68	0.05	-10.68
1990-2009	4.55	-15.36	-14.84	-20.60	-3.08	0.51	-2.21	-8.87
2005-2009	-7.04	-8.66	-16.42	-2.15	4.31	5.60	-5.67	1.23

RER Misalignment in ECOWAS, WAMZ and Cape Verde (cont'd)

ANNEES	PAYS DE LA ZMAO					Cap - Vert
	Gambia	Ghana	Guinea	Nigeria	Sierra Leone	
1990	116.12	75.16	8.43	2.50	25.44	26.26
1991	116.20	70.06	10.31	-4.87	26.99	6.87
1992	122.96	45.31	14.41	-19.32	12.55	-5.78
1993	137.40	27.68	20.24	-14.06	20.24	-25.55
1994	123.36	5.27	26.85	48.02	34.52	-28.20
1995	115.71	23.10	33.76	16.13	19.03	-27.64
1996	114.62	34.50	38.57	35.33	18.18	-34.48
1997	125.72	43.38	42.33	51.37	33.45	-45.12
1998	130.55	55.44	45.58	73.77	13.45	-48.85
1999	131.47	56.60	48.98	-9.91	32.42	-52.40
2000	127.69	4.61	52.95	-7.14	20.83	-56.63
2001	104.09	6.20	38.54	1.97	30.03	-58.39
2002	73.87	3.87	27.12	-0.15	12.52	-56.58
2003	29.40	0.55	17.45	-7.76	-5.48	-47.99
2004	30.12	-4.75	8.34	-8.32	-12.92	-40.93
2005	40.06	1.03	-0.77	2.47	-6.88	-39.83
2006	40.53	2.82	3.54	8.54	1.75	-40.33
2007	52.95	-1.76	8.74	5.94	6.16	-34.86
2008	59.37	-9.25	16.84	17.50	15.39	-33.53
2009	62.91	-16.09	29.41	30.46	-2.65	-31.88
1990-2009	92.76	21.19	24.58	11.12	14.75	-33.79
2005-2009	51.17	-4.65	11.55	12.98	2.75	-36.08

Liberalisation of capital account and current account

Controls or measures	WAEMU	Cape Verde	The Gambia	Ghana	Guinea	Liberia	Nigeria	Sierra Leone	ECOWAS (% of countries with no controls)
Capital transaction	Yes	Yes	No	Yes	Yes	Yes	Yes	Yes	12.5
Instruments of monetary and financial markets	Yes	Yes	No	Yes	Yes	No	Yes	Yes	25.0
Controls on derivatives and other instruments	Yes	No	No	Yes	No	No	No	N.A.	75.0
Credit transactions of residents	No	Yes	Yes	Yes	Yes	No	Yes	Yes	25.0
Direct investment (capital outflow)	Yes	Yes	No	Yes	No	No	No	No	62.5
Direct investment (capital inflow)	No	Yes	No	Yes	Yes	N.A.	No	Yes	50.0
Liquidation of direct investment	No	No	No	Yes	No	No	Yes	No	75.0
Real estate transactions (purchases by residents)	Yes	Yes	No	Yes	Yes	Yes	No	Yes	25.0
Personal capital transactions	Yes	Yes	No	Yes	Yes	No	Yes	No	37.5

Limits of open currency position	Yes	Yes	No	Yes	Yes	No	Yes	Yes	12.5
Specific provisions for investors	Yes	N.A.	No	No	No	No	No	Yes	75.0
Other controls imposed by the Securities Act	No	N.A.	No	No	N.A.	No	No	No	100.0
Joining the scheme of Article VIII of the IMF	June 1996 & Jan. 1997	(Jul. 2004)	21 Jan. 1993	2 Feb. 1994	17 Nov. 1995	N.A.	N.A.	14 Dec. 1995	23.5
Liberalisation status (%)	38.46	30.77	84.61	23.10	46.15	76.92	46.15	46.15	49.04

Financial Integration

Proliferation of branches of transnational banks:	Integration of existing stock exchanges:
Ecobank Transnational, UBA, Guarantee Trust Bank, Access Bank, First International Bank, Union Bank, Standard Bank, etc. The challenge is about cross-border banking supervision.	♦ Regional Stock Market (BRVM) in Abidjan ♦ Stock Exchange of Nigeria ♦ Stock Exchange of Ghana ♦ Stock Exchange of Sierra Leone ♦ Stock Exchange of Cape Verde

ECOWAS is taking action for the creation of an investment jurisdiction among member countries to ensure accelerated development of small and medium enterprises and attract foreign direct investment.

ECOWAS is developing a common investment code and a policy framework for regional investment to facilitate new investments through the elimination of cumbersome procedures.

The Conference of Heads of State and government adopted additional legislation on the rules of common investment market, and competition rules in December 2008 to accelerate cooperation in the key areas of trade, finance and investment to achieve the goal of an integrated economy.

Development of systems of payment

Satisfactory evolution of the SP within the ECOWAS.

The WAEMU has an integrated system of payment including:

♦ modernisation of the system of trading and settlement of transactions for large and small amounts with:

System of Automated Transfer and Settlements (STAR-UEMOA): RTGS

Automated Interbank Clearing (SICA-UEMOA)

♦ development of a sub-regional banking card system (electronic banking group and interbank electronic payment processing centre)

♦ strengthening sub-regional telecommunications infrastructure to ensure high quality services at an affordable price

Under the West Africa Monetary Zone (WAMZ), efforts are being made to bring payment systems of member states at the same level:

♦ Ghana and Nigeria are equipped with an operational system for RTGS. This system is being implemented in three other countries (The Gambia, Guinea and Sierra Leone) with funding from the African Development Bank (ADB).

♦ For checks, WAMZ has also adopted common norms and standards. Common rules on payment systems have also been developed and are being adopted.

♦ At the individual level, each member country is working hard to be in tune with recent developments in terms of payment systems.

WAMA is working to harmonise the zonal and national payment systems for consistency, interoperability and for future interconnectivity.

Harmonisation of monetary policy frameworks

WAMA is currently working on:

♦ A proposal for harmonising monetary policy frameworks on the basis of an assessment of existing systems within the region. This proposal will be submitted to the Committee of Experts during their regular meetings in late 2012.

♦ A study of the transmission mechanisms of monetary policies

♦ A study on the function of money demand.

Harmonising statistics on balance of payments

Preparation of three documents:

♦ In-depth diagnosis paper of current practices especially in terms of methodology, sources and data collection

♦ Paper for proposed harmonisation of concepts, sources and methodology

♦ A regional methodological guide for planning and achieving the desired harmonisation.

Harmonising the accounting and reporting framework for banks and other financial institutions

Measures are taken by all Central Banks within ECOWAS for the adoption of the IFRS (International Financial Reporting Standards) in all member countries.

Harmonising the regulatory and supervision framework of banks and other financial institutions

♦ Development of a benchmarking report of all national or sub-regional banking and financial laws in force within ECOWAS, identifying gaps and shortcomings

♦ Review of current arrangements governing the activity and supervision of banks and other financial institutions, based on the principles of Basel I and II

♦ Development of a proposal on procedures for harmonizing and a schedule for implementation.

Conclusion

Some progress has been made under the EMCP:

♦ Some ECOWAS countries have made great efforts to stabilise their economies and to harmonise their fiscal, monetary and financial policies

♦ The liberalisation of current and capital accounts has been advanced

♦ The draft of the second Zone (WAMZ) has made significant progress

♦ Some economies have very acceptable levels of convergence.

However, in West Africa, the ECOWAS needs to make more progress in other areas of regional integration for all countries participating in the monetary union to gain some interest in meeting their commitments. The monetary union will not thrive without the support of other policies and institutional arrangements, in addition to a spirit of solidarity between stakeholders. In conclusion, it appears that the expected benefits of the ECOWAS monetary union could outweigh the costs for various reasons.

FIRST STEPS TO CREATING THE NILO CURRENCY FOR AFRICA —Yash Tandon

Introduction

In June 2009, the Cheikh Anta Diop University invited me to write a paper for a symposium on the United States of Africa. In my paper, entitled 'Reclaiming Africa's self-reliance: federalism, economic development, science and technology', I suggested the creation of a non-convertible African currency called the 'nilo' (after the River Nile) to service purely intra-African trade.[1] I am not an expert on currency or monetary issues, nor is this a technical paper about how to create the nilo. I write as a generalist interested in Pan-African development toward, ultimately, an economic and political union of Africa.

In this paper, I argue that there is no country or region in the world that can enjoy real independence without owning and controlling its own money. Stated frankly, the proposition sounds dogmatic. But it is not. It is the reality of the present (and past) asymmetrical global economic and political systems. It is my view that in order to advance the cause of Pan-Africanism and for Africa to be able to speak effectively in the global fora, it is incumbent that it creates and controls its own currency. There are good economic reasons for this. But more significant than the economic reasons, are those connected with Africa's security and political independence in the current era of generalised warfare. The paper seeks to elaborate on this thesis.

---

1 . Throughout the paper I use the term nilo in place of 'African or continental currency'. The nilo could eventually be called by another name.

Is the nilo too fanciful an idea?

The suggestion of the nilo as a common currency for Africa is not a mere fantasy. In my 2009 paper, I gave the example of a common trading currency called the Unit of Account for PTA (UAPTA). It was created some 25 years ago, in August 1988, by the Preferential Trade Area of Eastern and Southern Africa (PTA) – now renamed COMESA.[2] The UAPTA was a mechanism for minimizing the use of hard currencies, such as the U.S. dollar and pound sterling. It also enabled the citizens of member states to travel within the region without having to use foreign currency (the UAPTA was then equivalent to one Special Drawing Right of the IMF). The PTA set up its own bank with capitalisation of $360 million including a $130 million reserve fund to support the operations of UAPTA clearing house.

However, less than a decade later, in June 1997, the UAPTA was discontinued. Why? The reasons are far from simple, for they are political and economic, external to Africa (including the World Bank- IMF imposed neoliberal policies), as well as internal (contradictions within the member countries). I cite UAPTA only because I know it first-hand (having used it myself), but there have been several such attempts (some failed, some successful) to create currencies in other parts of Africa. So the idea of an African continental or regional currency is not as outlandish or bizarre. It is a doable project, but admittedly a challenging one.

Limits of this paper

Before I go further I need to define the limits of our discussion in this paper. I do not go into the very exciting and innovative discussion about alternative currencies.

---

2. The Common Market for Eastern and Southern Africa (COMESA) consists mostly of countries of Eastern and Southern Africa, but also includes Egypt, Eritrea, Ethiopia, the DRC, Libya and Sudan. The COMESA has a population of about 400 million, and total GDP of about $360 billion.

Alternative mediums of exchange have existed through civilisations, and they exist today in many communities around the world. These are currencies that do not depend on money as a medium of exchange. These include, for example, exchange in the form of labour vouchers – exchange of labour services of equivalent (or roughly equivalent) values – and e-currencies that do not use the banking or traditional currencies for personal or business transactions. I do not go into these. Here we focus on the conventional definition of currency as fiduciary money, money that has the authority of the state to realise its value as a medium of exchange or as a store of value.

The thrust of the argument

My argument develops along the following lines:

1. I examine why Africa needs its own currency. I rate the political-strategic-security consideration as higher than the economic (though this is important, too) as the principal reason for Africa to create its own currency.

2. I argue that the present global financial/economic crisis has opened up an opportunity for Africa to take serious first steps to launch its own currency. However, the present neoliberal and neo-Keynesian policies to reform the global system are doomed to fail. Therefore, it is argued, Africa needs to take a far more radical approach.

3. I make some tentative suggestions on the first steps in the long journey to create an African currency that it owns and controls.

Why Africa needs its own currency

There are two main reasons why Africa needs to create and control its own currency – one, in the strategic-security-political domain, and the other in the economic domain. The discussion in most academic and policy circles revolves around the economic. This is not surprising. Money, credit, foreign exchange, market, currency, etc. are quintessentially economic categories. But, it is important to understand that economics is a blind academic discipline; it does not see, or at best it obfuscates, the political reality behind it. Dig deeper into this pseudo-science and you will find, hidden behind its categories and assumptions, political strategies and tactics of the old game of conquest and exploitation.

Economics is politics. The only reason I treat these as separate in this paper, and draw out narrowly defined economic arguments, is in order to engage those who deal with economic matters in the government ministries of trade and finance and in the academic discipline called economics. And so although I end this paper by suggesting certain measures (first steps) that appear to be economistic, it must be understood that behind my proposals lies a sound political argument, a critical argument for the times we live in.

There is another reason for going into the politics of economics, and this is ideology. Since about the mid-1970s, the world has been served a heavy dose of neoliberal ideology. It became even more imposing in claiming the status of science after the fall of the Berlin Wall and the demise of the Soviet alternative model. After 1989, the only game in town was neoliberal economics, whose policy prescriptions were presented as axiomatic, indeed as second nature to humanity's future growth and development. The walls of this ideology are finally falling asunder following the financial (economic) crisis, which broke surface in 2007-2008 triggered by the sub-prime housing scandal and virtual collapse of the global banking system, but which has been lurking for the past 30 years.

Of course, the old horse (neoliberalism) is still delivering solid kicks that still hurt the poor nations and the poor in all nations. Nevertheless, even as it is dying a slow death, its demise is now a historical certainty. This has opened the door to another ideology. Suddenly, as if from nowhere, we have neo-Keynesian economics (almost forgotten for 30 years) with its putative claim to be a social-democratic alternative to neoliberalism. This paper will not go into the sterile debate between the neoliberals and the neo-Keynesians. I mention this only in order to alert readers not to get caught up in this debate. What Africa needs is a much more radical approach, one that recognises that economics is politics by other means.

The political-strategic-security reasons for creating the nilo

A critical argument of this paper is that the post-9/11 world has triggered a new era of generalised warfare. We are living through a protracted war that could last through and beyond the present generation. In this evolving scenario whose future is far from clear, it behooves Africa to have its own currency in order to maintain a measure of independence and in order not to be dragged into other peoples' wars through monetary and currency manipulations.

Two questions arise: 1) What kind of war is it? and 2) What has war to do with having an independent currency? I will not dwell on the first question. It has complex physical, ideological-cum-religious and social-psychological dimensions. All I can say is that it is not like the two world wars of the last century, nor like the cold war that lasted for nearly 50 years to the end of the last century. We are living through another kind of war in a profoundly different situation – including a new kind of global awakening a new kind of resistance to the old power structures; a new kind of challenge to received dogmas and ideologies... But let me stop here; this is a subject for another discourse. The second question is more relevant to the subject at hand. Why should this war (whatever its character) be linked with the issue of Africa owning its own currency? What has one got to do with the other? This, too, is a complex matter, but its main outlines can be identified without too much difficulty.

All things change; everything is in flux. Nonetheless, there are certain things that change in content and form, but not in essence. Money is such a thing. Money has existed through time immemorial. It has changed in form and content, but essentially is a weapon of war both in peace and war times. We know how money and currency played a critical role in the colonial conquest of the Americas (the US and South America), Asia, and Africa. Nathan Rothschild, who virtually controlled the Bank of England famously said that 'he who controlled Britain`s money supply also controlled the British Empire'. European imperial-colonial countries (Holland, Portugal, Spain, England, France and Belgium) kept coinage out of the control of the colonies to prevent them from trading with one another. From Africa's own history, we know that the expansion of money and capital from 1880s led first to colonial conquest of Africa after the Berlin Conference of 1884–1885, and later to inter-imperial rivalry and the two world wars. Money played a critical role in wars and colonisation. One of the first things the new colonial masters did in the African colonies was to introduce the monopoly of their own currency systems. This hold over Africa of imperial currencies exists to this day; and Africa needs to break out of it.

What do the Punic Wars teach Africa?

Let us take a couple of examples from history first, for history is full of evidence of the connection between money and war. The role that money played in the three Punic Wars fought between Rome and Carthage between 264 and 146 BC (including the Battle of Tunis on the African soil) is well documented in history books. Rome used money as a weapon of war, but ironically, the ultimate destruction of Rome's money system in the final years of the Punic wars was one of the most critical factors that led finally to its own demise.

What does the American War of Independence teach Africa?

The experience of the English colonies of America (now the USA) is worth recalling for African readers. Pennsylvania (in the colonial period) created its own paper money in 1723 to assert its independence from the Empire, and interestingly it was the only colony that managed to prevent inflation that ravaged the other colonies, which were dependent on the English currency.[3] In 1764, however, England passed the Currency Act to curb issuance of colonial money. In 1766, Benjamin Franklin went to London to petition against it but was rejected by the imperial-colonial government.[4]

However, at the first Continental Congress in Philadelphia in May 1775, the revolutionary colonies decided to create their own currency called the "Continental Currency". During the war of American independence, the English tried to undermine the continental currency through massive counterfeiting as a weapon of war.[5] The American liberation warriors, despite English efforts to sabotage their currency, managed to finance the war, and in 1776 at the Declaration of Independence, the colonies legalised their new currency. Thus the US finally broke away from the imperial currency system. And this is what Africa needs to do.

This story has its own double irony, however. The same USA, by an ironical twist of history, is lording over the rest of the world today with its dollar power. Earlier, I observed that Rome used money as a weapon of war, but ironically, the ultimate destruction of Rome's money system in the final years of the Punic wars was one of

---

3 . An interesting aside is that in order to protect its independent currency, Pennsylvania inflicted heavy penalties on those engaged in counterfeiting, including cutting off of both ears on first offence and both limbs on later offences. This aside should not be interpreted to mean an implied encouragement to the present-day Sharia law, which is a domain outside my competence.

4 . Franklin had criticised the Austrian School of Economics – what Franklin ridiculed as the Austrian School of Economyths associated with Ludwig Von Mises – for their ignorance of monetary issues.

5 . They were out of the reach of Pennsylvania's "ear-cutters". Actually, the English set up printing presses aboard British ships in New York to flood the American money system with counterfeits.

the most critical factors that led to its own demise. This is the (inevitable) fate of the American empire too. That is why the US cannot allow a counter global currency, or to loosen its control over, for example, the IMF and its military wing, the North Atlantic Treaty Organization (NATO).

What does the current crisis in Europe teach Africa?

In our own times we have the experience of Greece struggling over the past several years to reclaim its sovereignty. Little did its people realise (indeed, they were never meaningfully consulted) that by replacing its currency (the drachma) with the euro, Greece would lose its ability to define and control its own economic policies; that it would lose its sovereignty. Now Greece is at the mercy of its EU partners, the European Development Bank, and the IMF.

Of course, it might be argued that Greece is unique, that this is not the experience of countries such as Germany, France or Sweden – these, too, have also abandoned their independent currency in favour of the euro without facing Greece-kind of crisis. This is partly true. But this argument has two sides to it. One is national and the other regional. Nationally, Germany, France and Sweden (the northern countries) have strong economies relative to, for example, Greece, Portugal, Spain and even Italy (the Mediterranean countries). The ancient wisdom that the strong tend to rule the weak is being played out in Europe between the northerners and the Mediterraneans. Regionally, what the Maastricht Treaty hoped to create was a strong, united Europe that could match the strength of the US and Japan. But a strong Europe, in turn, required that countries in the region surrender part of their sovereignty to the will of the collective in order to reap the long-term benefits of the collective strength that comes from unity. You sacrifice a bit of sovereignty nationally so as to gain more out of regional unity. There are thus two sides of the same coin – national and regional.

How does this analogy apply to Africa? It applies both in its national and regional contexts. There is no gainsaying that if African countries want to be able to talk with the rest of the world with a strong, united voice, each of them needs to surrender part of its sovereignty to the collective will of Africa. And here lies the real challenge. No African country is willing to do this – at least in the foreseeable future. The irony is that what African countries are not prepared to do in the African context, they have done so already in the global context. Currently, African countries have their sovereignty compromised not only in economic terms, but also in terms of political and security policies, by a historically imposed domination of the empire over the continent.

A distractive argument that we must deal with is that the empire does not exist; that Africa is now independent and Africans must not continue to lay blame on neocolonialism for all their ills. The second part of the above statement is partly true – African leaders too often hide behind the imperial skirts of their erstwhile masters to cover up their own weaknesses and frailties. But the first part – the point about the empire – is a reality that no amount of linguistic subterfuge can hide. The imperial reality is extant. It has changed its character from the days of direct colonialism, but it is present in all its force and vigour.

Europe is part of that empire. (I may add, parenthetically, that countries such as Sweden, Norway and Finland are also part of the empire – perhaps more benign but there should be no illusion on this score). Africa, on the other hand, is not yet independent. Africa in this sense is different from Europe. For example, it is true that Europe compromises its sovereignty on matters of security in Iraq, or Afghanistan or Syria to the will of the US – the most dominant player in NATO. But Europe does that for its own strategic and security interests. Also, Europe enjoys relative independence in matters related to for example, trade, investment and environmental policies that could be the envy of Africa. It is not without reason that in the face of the global economic crisis the Europeans are trying their best to preserve their independent currency (the euro), even at the cost of bringing weaker countries like Greece, Ireland and Portugal to toe the European line.

The Roman and American examples from the past, and the example of Greece and Europe in our own times, support three important conclusions:

1. Money is war by other means from antiquity to the present times.

2. Africa's independence and sovereignty are compromised by the historically imposed will of the empire over Africa. This imperial will is exercised through many channels – political, military, ideological and economic; through so-called development aid and, above all, through control over Africa's monetary system.

3. Africa can learn from the experience of the thirteen American colonies in the 1760s – break away from imperial currencies, and create its own. Africa must also learn from Europe's determination to hold on to the euro. The leading nations of Europe do not want to mortgage their future to the US dollar either in the economic domain or in the political-strategic-security domain.

The post-9/11 world has triggered a new era of generalised warfare, which is still in its early stages, whose evolution is still in the future. Money is playing an extremely important role in triggering and fuelling the wars in the Arab world. Syria is inundated with money from, for example, the US, Europe and their allies in the oil-rich Gulf countries. Also, in the case of Iran, one of the objectives of the NATO coalition is to weaken Iran's currency through massive embargo on its oil exports and escalated sanctions. Currencies are weapons of war, just like scud missiles and the drones. Africa must create an independent currency. The importance of this strategic objective cannot be exaggerated.

The economic reasons for creating the nilo

Earlier I argued that economics is political-economy masquerading as pseudo-science, or what Benjamin Franklin called economyths. The best examples of this are the neoliberal and the neo-Keynesian economics. I have also no doubt that whilst the Marxist method of dialectic materialism provides a better tool for analysis than the neoliberal or neo-Keynesian epistemologies, there is no such thing as Marxist economics or neo-Marxist economics. These are reductionist economistic distortions of what Marx wrote and fought for.

But let us not get into this ideological discourse. The economic argument for the nilo is made in order, to engage and to connect with people involved in academic and policy issues in Africa. We all agree that Africa has abundant natural and human resources, and that it needs to use these to get out of poverty and underdevelopment. Our disagreements or confusion are on the question of where we get investment capital to develop these resources. And this begs the question: Why is it that Africa creates a lot of added value in production but it still needs capital from outside?

This is a question that has been with us since the colonial times. Let me say that part of our confusion has been created by mirrors and magic lanterns created by the empire; these distort realities and turn them upside down. Let me illustrate this from the experience of my country – Uganda. Dani Nabudere, in *Imperialism and Revolution in Uganda*, has shown how during the colonial times, the surplus from Uganda, extracted out of peasant commodity production, became so large that a substantial part of it was exported to Britain.[6] In 1958, for example, of the £17.5 million deposited in Uganda banks £11.6 million was used in Uganda and the rest was sent to Britain. He quotes the colonial economic historian, Walter Newlyn, who wrote:

---

6 . Nabudere, D.W. (1980) *Imperialism and revolution in Uganda*, Onyx Press

The outstanding characteristic of this phase of their development (of the banks) was that they soon became able to collect deposits locally in excess to what they were able to utilize in the East African countries and these surplus funds they invested in London. The result was that for a long period of their history, these banks were actually involved in the process of exporting capital from the underdeveloped countries of East Africa for use in a developed country.[7]

In essence, nothing has changed from those days. Africa is still the net exporter of capital to the empire. Africa has got its political independence, but the system of production, trading and currencies remain more or less the same, except that the separate bilateral colonial rules (British, French, etc.) have been replaced by multilateral rule under the overall direction of the World Bank and the IMF. More than 50 years after their creation, these institutions of global economic governance, are still stubbornly controlled by the US-led empire. Under this multilateralised imperial regime, there is a net outflow of both resources and money capital from Africa, and figures bear this out. Africa pays out more than it gets. There is enormous value added in production in Africa, especially in commodities, and yet Africa retains an insignificant share of this value. Again, figures even from sources within the IMF and the World Bank bear this out.

Why this is so should surprise nobody. It is not a result of something insidious (although this too, as later explained); it is largely because this is how the system works globally. There is no automatic levelling down (or trickle down) process at the international (or for that matter at the national) level. Asymmetries are built into the workings of the system. Power and wealth concentrations are inherent to the system. Those who have accumulated wealth through various forms of rent seeking acquire more of what they have, thus exacerbating the rich-poor gap both within and

---

7 . Ibid. p.65, citing Newlyn W.T. (1972) Money in an African Context, Oxford, p.43

between nations. Over time, however, some insidious practices have indeed become part of the system, such as speculation in commodities and in the foreign exchange and derivatives markets, much of which are openly fraudulent, and enjoying a large measure of impunity.

Oiling this vast system of what amounts to theft is the money system. It is for this reason that many writers have given a specific name to this era of capitalism, namely a system of financialised capitalism; a system where making money out of money is rewarding speculators and bankers more than those involved in actual production; where stocks are floated onto the money market and leveraged through derivatives that have no relation to the value of hard, tangible, assets; where governments (mainly in the US and Europe) are engaged in printing money (confusingly called by the technically beguiling phrase Quantitative Easing or QE to fool the masses). This is actually to enable their banks to balance their books, which have fake (toxic) assets. This is the real world of present-day capitalism.

Why the neo-Keynesian reformist solution is an illusion

The demise or near-demise of the neoliberal paradigm has opened the door to several reformist solutions – some still within the same paradigm, some outside of it. One of the latter is the neo-Keynesian reformist solution, named after the English economist, John Maynard Keynes, a brilliant bureaucrat who showed one possible way out of the depression of the 1930s. Keynes was engaged on the British side in the negotiations leading to the creation of the Bretton Woods institutions (the World Bank and the IMF), except that he lost out to the more powerful Americans. The British were already in post-war decline. Nonetheless, Keynesian economics flourished in some social-democratic milieu until buried under the avalanche of neoliberalism in the 1970s. More recently it has resurrected itself in some left reformist circles.

I shall not go into this theory. What concerns us here is the application of neo-Keynesian economics to the present financial-economic crisis. One of its most brilliant contemporary advocates is the American Nobel Laureate, Joseph Stiglitz, who headed the commission of experts set up at in September 2009 by the United Nations General Assembly, to study the financial crisis in depth and make recommendations. I have summarised the findings and recommendations of that commission elsewhere.[8] The report contained some of the best ideas that money can buy on how to reform the international financial architecture to prevent future occurrences of the crises.

The point to underscore is that nothing is heard of the report. Not a single of its 10 major recommendations has been followed up. Why not? A quick answer, without getting into sordid details, is that the ruling classes – and the entire paraphernalia of the capitalist system, controlled by an un-regulateable mafia of bankocrats, kleptocrats, speculators and state bureaucrats – have absolutely no interest in reforming a system of which they are the principal beneficiaries.

The crisis of the dominant system is an opportunity for Africa

The struggle for liberation from the hold of the empire is a long struggle. Much of what is happening in the Arab world is part of that scenario. Africa too is embroiled in several wars within the continent, whose causes are deeply rooted in its colonial past, with lingering ethnic-religious-class and political-economic dynamics of power and resource distribution at their core. Notwithstanding, at the political-economic level, the failure of the neoliberal and reformist solutions to the global multiple crises opens the door for more innovative and radical thinking on the part of African activist intellectuals and grass- roots social movements.

8. Tandon, Y. (2012) 'Economic Policies response to the financial crisis: a view from the South', presented at conference: Sustainable Development Alternatives: how to change the social paradigm focused on human being and nature, Quito, June.

I have also floated some ideas along these lines, especially during my tenure as executive director of SEATINI (Southern and Eastern African Trade Information and Negotiations Institute), 1997–2004; and then as executive director of the South Centre, 2005–2009. I have argued, as have Samir Amin, Dani Nabudere and others before me, that it is imperative that Africa and the countries of the South decouple – or delink – themselves from the crisis-prone system of the North. A serious debate is urgently needed in Africa between its political leaders, its academic and intellectual community, and its civil society; and above all, between all of these and the movements of the people on the ground who are at the receiving end of all ill-conceived policies carried out in their name. This is the democratic transparency that is needed, not the top-down financial and banking 'transparency' of the G8, the G20, the IMF, the World Bank, the European Union, and the OECD. This is not to underestimate the gravity of the problems that face Africa and the South in trying to work out an alternative model of a monetary and financial system. But a long journey is never started without taking the first step?

Putting the issue of nilo in the broader context of a 10-point strategic programme of action

Africa is not alone in venturing on this long struggle. Efforts are afoot also in other parts of the South. Among such efforts, I would cite the work of the Ecuadorian political-economist, Pedro Páez, as offering some of the best ideas on the subject of money systems and currencies. In the above cited paper I have summarised his ideas.

So here in point form are some of the critical steps that might be taken – in parallel or sequentially, depending on the circumstances - to undertake a radical reform not only of the financial and currency system, but also of Africa's general orientation to the rest of the world. Obviously, the 10-point program of action suggested below is not a one-day affair, and certainly not something that can be carried out by a single

African country. It can be done at the continental level by for example the African Union, or the Economic Commission for Arica (ECA); and/or (simultaneously or in sequence) at the regional level involving regional organisations such as COMESA and ECOWAS.

1. Break trade barriers between African countries and create customs unions, and encourage those that are already doing this (ECOWAS and EAC) to expedite their efforts.

2. Create regional monetary arrangements (RMAs), including flexible regional bloc exchange rate regimes (ERR), and the creation of regional currencies. It is not necessary at this stage to create fully-fledged regional currencies, such as the euro. What is immediately doable is the creation of regional trading currencies, such as the uapta. The uapta can be given a new lease of life along revised format and structures, but retaining its potential to evolve into a regional currency.

3. Create regional banks and community banks funded entirely out of savings generated within Africa and therefore independent of aid or capital from outside.

4. Aim in the long run to turn banks into post offices. Money should be owed by people and handed over to post offices to manage issuance of credit and servicing loans for a fee. The Grameen Bank in Bangladesh started out well because it was based on the above principle, but it got corrupted along the way on account of infiltration by the dominant money system and the World Bank.

5. Review all the donor-driven agreements (for example, those with the IMF, the World Bank, USAID and the European Commission). Some of these agreements need to be scrapped and others fundamentally changed or re-negotiated. This might require a certain level of expertise in evaluating the economic, political and legal dimensions of these agreements, as well as some financial resources.

6. Of critical significance are development aid agreements, the bilateral investment treaties (BITs), and the free trade agreements, such as the economic partnership agreements (EPAs), now being negotiated under extreme pressure from the European Union. There should be an immediate embargo on further negotiations of the EPAs, in order to buy time for Africa to consider its options.

7. African political and grassroots leaders should, as early as possible, link up with countries in other parts of the South (for example, the Alba counties in Latin America and the ASEAN countries) in order to exchange ideas and methodology of working out a government-to-government and people-to-people South-South strategy for a more radical approach to the financial and economic crises.

8. At the global level, Africa (and the global South) is better placed to work through the G77 group rather than through the G20, which has been co-opted into an apparatus set up and dominated by the G7 countries.

9. The global financial system remains extremely fragile. And so, whilst working toward an alternative system, Africa (and the South) might create a co-coordinating mechanism to monitor the volatility of the financial system, and to create fire-walls as buffers from its effects. The use of national currencies (as between China and Iran and some African countries) is an example of de-coupling, but there are other firewall mechanisms that might be put in place.

10. Above all, African leaders should be careful not to allow big powers to fight their proxy wars in Africa as happened during the Cold War. The African Union and African leaders should apply maximum efforts to defuse the situations in, for example, Somalia and Mali. Insulate these situations from infiltration by external big power interests, and seek peaceful solutions that are wholly African.

Conclusion

There is no country or region in the world that can enjoy real independence without owning and controlling its own money. A country or region that has no control of its money is never going to be independent. Africa's independence and sovereignty are compromised by the historically imposed will of the empire. This imperial will is exercised through: political, military, ideological, and economic channels, such as development aid and imposed monetary and currency controls.

This broad historical and ontological landscape of Africa forms the context in which the continent's response to the financial crisis must be addressed. There is a widely shared consensus that the financial crisis is systemic, and an outcome of the current era of financialised capitalism; a phase where unproductive financial and speculative capital has stumped productive capital. For several decades the countries of the South have been subjected to austerity economics and financial bail outs by the IMF and the donors. As it turns out, and as the Greek experience further demonstrates, the bail outs were for the globalised banking system and not for the people of the South. The IMF's stabilisation project was always a fraud, a 'Mission IMF-ossible'.

This is the economic reason for Africa to seek its own path to recovery from the present crisis, and the best way is for it to decouple itself from the crisis-ridden and crisis-perpetuating empire-dominated economic system, and to create a system that it owns and controls. But deeper than the economic reasons are the political-strategic-security reasons. A new kind of war began after 9/11. This war could be protracted and evolve in unpredictable ways in the generations to come. Africa needs peace for another two or three generations to get out of its poverty and underdevelopment, and an independent globally non-tradable currency would be one of the major ingredients of the peace it needs.

.

COMMENT ON YASH TANDON'S PRESENTATION
Lansana Keita

Yash Tandon's paper is an interesting one in that it looks at Africa's economic development potential in the correct way. Most articles and books on African economic development, whether written by Westerners or Africans, generally build their models on the monetary and political status quo. The main concerns are growth and privatisation, both inspired by the neo-liberal ideology. There is no recognition of the fact that growth by itself offers little insight into the sociological structures of African society. Gini coefficients reveal much more than mere growth, yet they hardly figure in pronouncements about growth. There is also little recognition that for purposes of capital formation, governments, if efficiently run, are better able than private corporations to advance the cause of development.

Yash Tandon's main point is that 'there is no country or region in the world that can enjoy real independence without owning and controlling its own money'. The reasons for emphasising this point are that it is not only an economic issue, but also one 'connected with Africa's security and political independence in the present turbulent world of generalised warfare that might last beyond the present generation'.[9]

Tandon's recommendations for the African 'nilo' are well taken in a period when Africa's multiple economies represent the least developed in the world. Most of the continent's 54 nations are small – with populations of less than 15 million people and little capital infrastructure, a necessity for economic development.

---

9 . Tandon, Yash (2012) 'First steps to creating the "Nilo" currency for Africa', Arcade/Codesria Conference, Dakar.

The 2011 Human Development Index formulated by the United Nations offers evidence that matters are indeed at a critical stage. Of the 186 countries surveyed and ranked according to indices, such as life expectancy, years of education, gender equity and access to health care, most of the countries in the fourth tier ('low development') are on the African continent. Even countries that have substantial deposits of petroleum, such as Gabon and Equatorial Guinea, rank no higher than medium development, in spite of their small populations. Nigeria and Angola, despite their bountiful natural resources including petroleum, are unfortunately in the lowest rung of the 46 nations on the Human Development Index. Of the 46 countries in the 'low development' category, 36 are in Africa.

Certainly, Tandon is on the right track to argue that a more compact Africa with nations bound together by common currencies is the optimal way forward. The UAPTA (Unit of Account for the Preferential Trade Area of Southern and Eastern Africa) offered an example of how things could be different with cooperation and regional integration founded on a common medium of exchange.

Tandon elaborates on his point that Africa needs its own currency for both economic and political reasons. Although most of the discussion focuses on economic issues, Tandon ranks the political-strategic-security issue higher than the economic, and 'the principal reason for Africa to create its own currency'. The reason for this, according to Tandon, is that economics as a discipline is essentially political economy. He is correct on this. Economics is always intertwined with politics, even as it pretends to be an objective social science. In a world of post-9/11 generalised warfare, Africa needs its own autonomous currencies, because history shows that nations in conflict often target one another's currencies. And when a nation does not control its own currency, it has already lost the political-economic battle.

I must however make a theoretical point concerning the discipline of economics. Political economy was transformed into economics or economic science not since the fall of the Berlin Wall, but long before that during the days of Neville Keynes (J.M. Keynes' father) and Alfred Marshall in Britain. In France, Leon Walras was after the same goal to transform political economy into a 'positive science.' This positive science became known as neoclassical economics, which, in turn, became neoliberalism, in practice on account of its central ideological point that market economics in the form of maximum privatisation should be the goal of economics.

Given the ongoing economic crisis, neoliberalism, as Tandon pointed out, is somewhat tarnished these days, and Keynesianism has witnessed a kind of rebirth in the Anglo-Saxon world. but all of the nations of continental Europe have modeled their post-Second World War economies principally on the Keynesian model. Norway, Sweden and Finland are good examples. (Sweden is not a member of the Eurozone). The governments of these countries are heavily involved in their economies. But regardless of these points, Africa needs a 'much more radical approach'.

Tandon pays attention to the fact that African nations are less inclined to give up sovereignty for the greater collective good. Yet, this has been done in the case of Europe with the euro. China, which has a variety of cultures and is more populous than the whole of Africa, has a single currency. Russia, the world's largest nation also has a single currency. The US is a federation of some 50 states, some which had their own currencies at one time—as pointed out by Tandon. They eventually gave up such currencies for the sake of single currency, signifying a collective national will. So, why not Africa?

Tandon's claim that the idea of African nations compromising their sovereignties by choosing a single currency is shown to be problematic because African nations themselves are still beholden to their ex-metropolises in particular, and to the Euro-

American world-led by the U.S. in general. Decades ago, the dependency school of Prebisch, Furtado, Dos Santos, Gunder Frank, and Samir Amin recognised that there was an ongoing dependency between the ex-colonies and their metropolises, which was described according to the twin concepts of centre and periphery. It is in this context that one could speak of the neocolonial paradigm and its impact on Africa's economics and politics.

The problem concerning the lack of unity and collective will among Africa's nations would seem to derive from the idea of false political consciousness and the international class role that the post-colonial African bourgeoisie plays in the international arena. This bourgeoisie is not an authentic bourgeoisie in the Western sense of the term. According to Frantz Fanon in his celebrated Wretched of the Earth, the pro-independence political parties and groups quickly shelved their Pan African ideology and African unity and replaced them with a narrow and venal nationalism at independence[10]

The national bourgeoisies of Africa are mere replacements for the colonial administrative classes, and being deprived over the colonial decades of the material goods manufactured in the West now go after these items with great gusto. They consume but they don't produce. As Fanon put it: 'the national middle class, which takes power at the end of the colonial regime, is an underdeveloped middle class. It has practically no economic power... In its narcissism, the national middle class is easily convinced that it can advantageously replace the middle class of the mother country'[11] Such a middle class has refused to commit class suicide, as Amilcar Cabral once recommended, and according to Fanon 'put itself to school with the people: in other words, to put at the people's disposal the intellectual and technical capital it has snatched when going through the colonial universities'[12]

10 . Fanon (1968) [1961] The Wretched of the Earth, New York. See the chapter titled 'The pitfalls of national consciousness'.
11 . Ibid. p.149.
12 . Ibid. p 150

This narrow nationalism put in place to ensure that the state properties and privileges created during the colonial era were monopolised by the new classes, led Fanon to note the following: 'We may understand why keen-witted international observers have hardly taken seriously the great flights of oratory about African unity, for it is true that there are so many cracks in that unity visible to the naked eye that it is only reasonable to insist that all these contradictions ought to be resolved before the day of unity can come.'[13] Fanon wrote such words many years ago and the wait is still on for that 'day of unity'.

A precondition for such unity is very few or a unique African currency along the lines of Tandon's 'nilo'. Events have not been encouraging, because ethnic strife and narrow nationalisms have been the order the day since the days of nominal independence. South Africa moved away from its promising slogan of Ubuntu to ethnic pogroms against migrant Africans from neighbouring countries. The riots of May 2008 are cases in point. The ethnic and religious conflicts in Nigeria and Congo are also known internationally. The same for Kenya, Guinea, Sudan, Rwanda and elsewhere.

Is it human nature or mainly false consciousness? I want to believe it is just false consciousness because humans become what they become not by instinct but by social conditioning. In this regard, education, in terms of African history, politics, and economics, is important. It is for this reason that the major impediment to African unity in terms of currencies is not the power of the Euro-American world itself, but the neocolonial African comprador bourgeoisies. Such classes lack the will for change on account of their material interests and the class roles they play. It is for the people in interaction with the committed intellectuals that will bring about change. They maintain their class dominance by way of the control of their national currencies – all very weak and non-convertible internationally.

---

13 . Ibid. p. 164

The neocolonial bourgeoisies protect their class interests in terms of their approach to the education meted out to the masses. Very few universities in Africa make available to their students in mandatory classes of instruction the works of important thinkers, such as Cheikh.Anta Diop, Frantz Fanon, Albert Memmi, Kwame Nkrumah, Amilcar Cabral and others. Even for the general public, there are few publishing houses in Africa that regularly reprint Diop, Fanon, Nkrumah, Cabral, etc. The reason is that with such a kind of instruction the narrow nationalisms of the myriad states of Africa would be threatened.

In sum, only the masses and committed intellectuals can push for, and eventually, implement the idea of Pan Africanism in terms of a single currency, as argued for by Tandon in his paper. But what would be the features of such a currency? It would have exactly the same features as the dollar and euro. It would be convertible, though Tandon argues that such a currency should not be convertible and be on close exchange rate parity with such currencies. It would mean too, that African nations would demand payment for their exported goods in terms of this single currency. There would be no need to find dollars or other so-called hard currencies to engage in international trade.

WITHER THE FRANC ZONE IN AFRICA?

www.ingramcontent.com/pod-product-compliance
Lightning Source LLC
Chambersburg PA
CBHW070355290526
45790CB00004B/1502